IMAGES
of America

THE UNIVERSITY OF CALIFORNIA MUSEUM OF PALEONTOLOGY

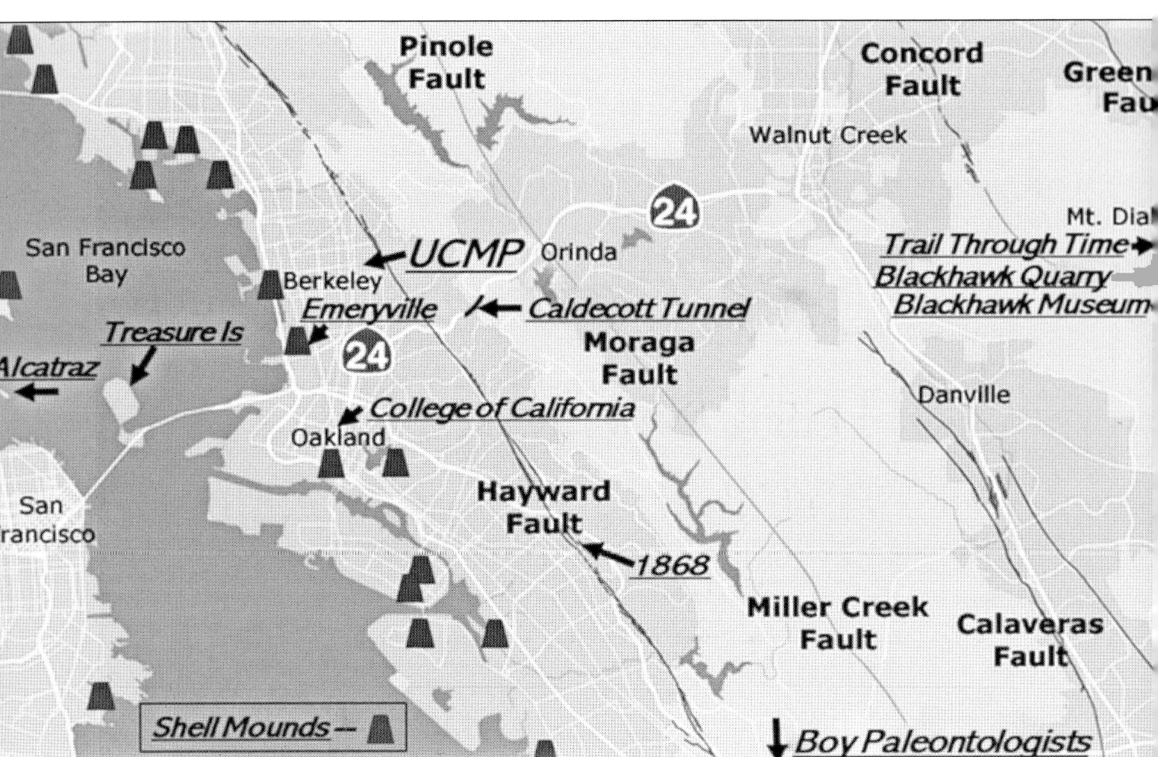

This map of the East Bay region shows the locations of the University of California Museum of Paleontology (UCMP) and places nearby where University of California (UC) paleontologists have worked. (Author's collection.)

On the Cover: In 1899, Prof. John C. Merriam initiated the first UC fossil expedition to the John Day region of Oregon. The team included, from left to right, Frank C. Calkins, mineralogy student; Loye Holmes Miller, Merriam's student; Merriam; and Leander S. Davis, an Oregon guide. They explored the deposits and collected fossils for later study. UCMP paleontologists continue to make trips to John Day. (Courtesy of the University of California Museum of Paleontology.)

IMAGES
of America

THE UNIVERSITY OF CALIFORNIA MUSEUM OF PALEONTOLOGY

Jere H. Lipps

ISBN 978-1-4671-0808-9

Published by Arcadia Publishing
Charleston, South Carolina

Printed in the United States of America

Library of Congress Control Number: 2021952355

For all general information, please contact Arcadia Publishing:
Telephone 843-853-2070
Fax 843-853-0044
E-mail sales@arcadiapublishing.com
For customer service and orders:
Toll-Free 1-888-313-2665

Visit us on the Internet at www.arcadiapublishing.com

The University of California Museum of Paleontology logo consists of its acronym with an ammonite fossil in blue and gold (UC's official colors) representing the "C." The museum is usually called "UCMP" and is referred to that way in publications. The logo was designed by David Smith, UCMP archivist, in 1995. (Courtesy of the University of California Museum of Paleontology.)

CONTENTS

Acknowledgments

For the last 34 years, I lived UCMP's history as faculty curator (1988–2022) and past director (1989–1998). Even before then, I interacted with UCMP and its people. From these interactions, I learned so much from so many people, from undergraduates to chancellors, that I cannot acknowledge them here except for those who were or are directly involved with paleontology at Berkeley. Charles Marshall, current director, provided support, discussion, access to archives, copyrighted materials, and UCMP information. Mark Goodwin, assistant director (retired), and Dave Smith, museum archivist, assisted in acquiring images and information without which I could not have done this book. I thank the late faculty curators William Berry, William A. Clemens, J. Wyatt Durham, F. Clark Howell, and Donald Savage for discussions in the past. The current faculty curators and associates—Walter Alvarez, Anthony Barnosky, Roy Caldwell, Seth Finnigan, Carole Hickman, Leslea Hlusko, David Lindberg, Juan Liu, Cynthia Looy, Kevin Padian, Paul Renne, Doris Sloan, Jack Tseng, and James Valentine—helped in many unique ways. Judy Scotchmoor, assistant director (retired), and Lisa White, assistant director, discussed accomplishments on outreach efforts; educational training; and diversity, equity, and inclusion. Museum scientists Ashley Dineen, Diane Erwin, Kenneth Finger, Pat Holroyd, and Howard Hutchinson hold special views of UCMP, which they afforded me. Lorraine Casazza, Chris Mejia, Sarah Rieboldt, Brian Simison, Robin Walker, and Colleen Whitney aided in a variety of ways. Former students Susan Goldstein (PhD, 1984), Mary McGann (PhD, 2004), David Polly (PhD, 1993), and Sally Walker (PhD, 1988) discussed UCMP when they were there, Joseph LeConte's history in Georgia, or provided images. I was privileged to talk to earlier students of paleontology at Berkeley: Loye Holmes Miller (PhD, 1912) at UCLA from 1960 to 1967, Vertress VanderHoof (PhD, 1935) at the Santa Barbara Museum of Natural History 1960–1961, Ruben Stirton (PhD, 1940) at UCMP in 1962, Edward Mitchell (PhD, 1967) in the field and labs for many years, and museum scientist Sam Welles (PhD, 1940) at UCMP in the 1990s. Joyce Blueford, M.A. Fedonkin, E. Landing, M. Langer, and J. Penkethman explored events and fossil sites with me. Susie Lipps gathered information about Joseph LeConte's life at Woodmanston Plantation and the University of Georgia, information about his relatives and slaves, and found critical images. I thank all these people more than I can express here. These memories kindled other leads and made this book all the more interesting to write. This book is a selective overview of UCMP history designed to spark an interest in paleontology and UCMP. More details and images can be seen at ucmp.berkeley.edu.

Throughout the text, "mya" refers to millions of years ago, or millions of years old.

INTRODUCTION

Paleontology is the study of ancient life through fossils ranging from bacteria to humans, extending back to the Precambrian 3.5 billion years ago. Such fossils are collected in the field, curated, and studied at UCMP, a research, education, and outreach center of UC Berkeley, in paleontology, sedimentary geology, evolutionary biology, systematics, molecular biology, and, increasingly, conservation and environmental biology. Organisms with skeletons—bones, shells, tests, spicules—fossilize commonly, whereas those with soft parts fossilize mostly as impressions. Behavior is revealed in tracks, trails, burrows, and coprolites (fossil excrement). Fossils provide evidence for the history of the land and sea through studies of climate change, ancient oceanography, plate tectonics, and paleoecology. Paleontologists say, "the present is the key to the past" and while that is true, the opposite is even more important: "the past is the key to the present *and* the future," for paleontology provides a history of the present and strong inferences about the future. History matters in natural and human endeavors.

Paleontology also contributed to industries searching for oil, coal, and other resources. The petroleum industry, in particular, relied on fossils in oil exploration. Petroleum changed the way we live and work; our societies would be quite different without the hundreds of products that come from oil as well as the degradation of the Earth, the warming of the atmosphere and oceans, and severe impacts on the original and subsequent inhabitants of the land they use. Paleontologists must recognize and acknowledge these aspects of the past as work continues to rectify these problems.

Paleontology has a public face too. Dinosaurs are particularly popular in movies, books, television, and museums and have entertained billions of people across the globe. UCMP also has its own dinosaur on display—a *Tyrannosaurus rex*. Dinosaurs starred in early movies—*Prehistoric Peeps* (1905), a four-minute cartoon, and *Gertie the Dinosaur* (1914), a 12-minute animated film. Dozens of dinosaur movies have appeared since and will certainly continue. *Jurassic Park* in 1993, seen by at least two billion people, topped them all. Every little kid knows all about dinosaurs. Dinosaurs, in fact, got many people started in science.

UCMP's mission is the development, care, and utilization of a complex collection of fossils and related materials. The collection contains fossils of every major lineage of life, from nearly every geological time period, and from sites worldwide. UCMP has more fossils than any other university and most museums—millions of specimens, hundreds of thousands numbered and curated, and many others still to be prepared. About 40,000 specimens, illustrated or documented in the scientific literature, are cataloged. UCMP has about half a million specimens of modern organisms, for paleontologists need comparative material and genetic analyses of living forms to better understand the relationships, ecology, and function of fossils. These collections were started in the mid-1800s, long before the museum was organized, and they have grown ever since. UCMP has laboratories for preparation, illustration, chemical and isotope analysis, and genetic sequencing. Teaching collections, developed and maintained by UCMP, are used in freshmen to graduate courses. UCMP's collection is full of fossils that reveal factual stories about life of the past. These stories have been and will be unraveled by UCMP paleontologists. So far, it only has fossils from Earth, but when ancient life is discovered on another planet, UCMP will collect that too.

A director leads UCMP. Faculty curators are professors in academic departments who teach with, advise, assist, contribute to, and use UCMP in various ways. Museum scientists care for the collections. Assistant directors oversee the curation process, outreach programs, and diversity, equity, and inclusion initiatives. All these people do research, teaching, and outreach with the collections. UCMP supports graduate and undergraduate students earning their degrees in an academic department. They study and add to the collections for their dissertations and theses. Visiting scholars come to work in the collections for their research projects.

UCMP's history is long and complex, involving more than 600 people over 170 years. Indigenous people built large mounds of shells, bones, sand, and mud along the edges of the San Francisco Bay that were studied by UC paleontologists. Although these Chochenyo-speaking Ohlone originally lived in tribes and villages, those relationships were destroyed by Spanish missionaries beginning around 1790. When Mexico gained independence from Spain in 1821, it granted to its citizens huge areas of land formerly occupied by Ohlone. The United States also wanted the land and warred with Mexico (1846–1848) over it. Fossils (1843) and gold (1848) were discovered in California. The ensuing 1849 Gold Rush indicated that California had great mineral wealth, and it was granted statehood in 1850. The legislature needed a geological survey to assess this wealth. These surveys also found fossils, which formed the basis for the UCMP collection. The University of California was created in 1868 on ancient Ohlone lands purchased from the College of California where the first UC classes were taught from 1869 to 1873. The faculty was small (10) as was the (entirely male) student body (42). The following year, women were admitted as students, among the first ever to be educated in an American university.

John and Joseph LeConte were hired in 1868 to teach physics and geology, natural sciences, and botany. They came with high recommendations from the Eastern science community. Born on a plantation in Georgia, their interest in science came from their experience in the natural habitats nearby and their father's scientific interests and teaching, especially botany. Joseph was an inspiring and beloved teacher at UC.

John C. Merriam, a LeConte student, later studied paleontology with the famous paleontologist Karl A. von Zittel in Munich, Germany, and returned to start a comprehensive paleontology program at UC. Annie Alexander, a wealthy woman with interests in the outdoors and its organisms past and present, took Merriam's lecture in 1900 and began to support paleontology with funding, expeditions, and negotiations with the UC administration. In 1909, she helped establish the Department of Paleontology, and in 1921, the Museum of Paleontology. Faculty, staff, and students have since made UC paleontology world famous with their research and teaching.

While Joseph LeConte promoted teaching and collection of fossils, paleontology, and natural history, as well as the development of UC for its initial 30 years, he also had a dark side—he was an unapologetic racist who believed that the white race was superior to the black race, as expressed in his writings and lectures. He also believed that women could not deal with practical problems, such as voting, like men could, and that they should take care of children and the home. These views are now offensive and not acceptable in a modern university or society. Places and things named for LeConte therefore have been unnamed or renamed. UCMP also rejects and aims to rectify these views through understanding its history; acknowledging the impacts; developing policies and activities that ameliorate the past situations through inclusion of everyone regardless of race, ethnicity, or any other characteristics; providing a safe workplace; and valuing and respecting the role everyone plays in the museum.

The University of California Museum of Paleontology at Berkeley sits on the territory of xučyun (Huichin), the ancestral and unceded land of the Chochenyo-speaking Ohlone people, the successors of the sovereign Verona Band of Alameda County. This land was and continues to be of great importance to the Muwekma Ohlone tribe and other familial descendants of the Verona Band.

One

Roots of UCMP

UCMP's history is deeply rooted in the peopling of the San Francisco Bay region. People from Asia arrived in California about 13,000 years ago when the sea level was 400 feet lower than now and the coastline was 30 miles off the Golden Gate. The bay was a pair of wooded river valleys. The sea reached the Golden Gate 8,000 years ago, and people lived along the coast. Sea level rose until about 4,000 years ago when the bay was filled. Ohlone villages covered the region with a population estimated at 20,000. Their Huichin tribe lived along the East Bay shore and harvested shellfish, birds, and sea mammals, building huge mounds of shells, bones, and sediment for 3,700 years. UC paleontologists excavated and studied these mounds from 1902 to 1928.

The Ohlones' lives were changed forever by the arrival of Spanish missionaries in the 1770s who converted them to Christianity, claimed the land for Spain, and gave the tribe diseases. Ohlone were taken into the missions where they raised crops and cattle and learned Spanish ways. With their removal from land they believed they were part of, the tribes, villages, and families broke up and lost their traditions. In 1820, Pablo Vicente de Solá, the last governor of Spanish California, gave a land grant, Rancho San Antonio, of 44,800 acres to Luís María Peralta for his 40 years of service to Spain. The grant included 8,000 cattle and 2,000 horses, as well as the land now occupied by UC and UCMP.

John C. Fremont explored Mexican California in 1843, finding the first fossils in California. He led troops in the Mexican-American War. It ended in 1848, and the Southwest and California were ceded to the United States. With the 1849 Gold Rush, people came from everywhere, and Californians planned for statehood, which Congress granted in 1850. The state placed bounties on Native Americans to clear the way. Geological surveys were organized to explore for mineral riches, and fossils were collected that formed the basis for the UCMP collections.

Spanish missionaries established 30 missions in Baja California beginning in 1683, and in 1769, Father Serra led Franciscans to Alta California, establishing 21 missions from San Diego north to Sonoma. Missions were built around the San Francisco Bay at Santa Clara, San Francisco, and near San José. Mission San José (shown above in 1860) was founded on June 11, 1797, and was the 14th mission in Alta California. People from the Ohlone tribes were brought to this mission to work in agriculture, ranching, and building and to attend church and educational services. Ohlone people at Mission San José danced with decorated bodies for the painting below by German scientist George von Langsdorff in 1806. Today's Ohlone Muwekma tribe consists of people from the Bay Area whose ancestors lived and worked at Mission San José. (Above, courtesy of Library of Congress; below, courtesy of the Bancroft Library.)

Huichin tribe shell mounds at Emeryville, West Berkeley, and Richmond contained skeletal remains, tools, bones, and innumerable shells of oysters, mussels, and clams. For more than 3,700 years, the Huichins lived on them, eating millions of meals and disposing of the remains, thus building the mounds. UC and UCMP acknowledge and honor these sacred lands and those people and their descendants. (Author's collection.)

By the 1920s, the mounds were gone, flattened for industry and commerce, and the shells quarried for fertilizer and cement without concern for the people who built them. The Bay Street shopping center and hotel were built over the remains of the Emeryville Mound in 1999–2003. The developer scaled back the project and provided funds to build a memorial consisting of a model of the mound (pictured) and a series of granitic slabs inscribed with information about the ancestors of the Ohlone people who lived on it for millennia and the significance the mound holds for the Ohlone of today. (Author's collection.)

Several Huichin shell mounds were located near Berkeley. UC paleontologist J.C. Merriam, interested in the Emeryville shell mound, hired N.C. Nelson and M. Uhle in 1902 to assist in his study. Nelson located 427 mounds around the San Francisco Bay Area while Uhle excavated at Emeryville. (Author's collection.)

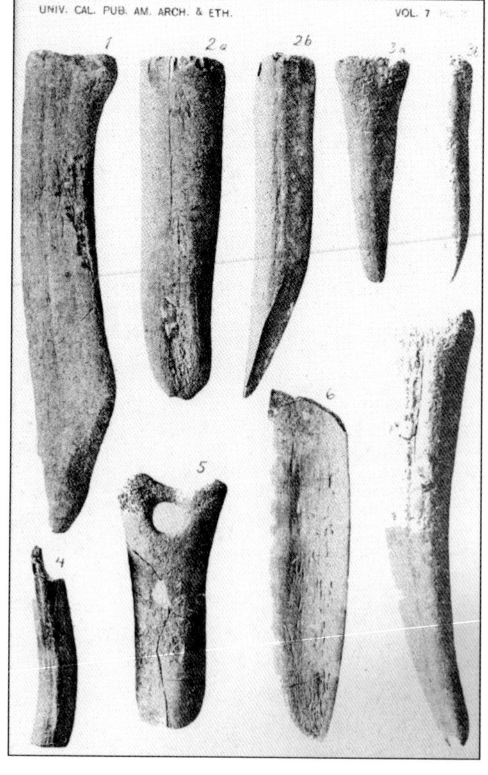

Uhle found bones, burials, and tools made from the bones of larger mammals. Hildegarde Howard, who earned her doctorate degree from UC Berkeley in 1928, studied the bird bones, determining from species in different levels that people occupied the mounds seasonally during the winter and early summer. (Author's collection.)

John C. Fremont (1813–1890, right) led five expeditions into Alta California from 1842 to 1853. Kit Carson (1809–1868, below) guided three of the expeditions. On his 1843 expedition, Fremont found fossils and arranged for their description. In Mexican California, Fremont advocated taking land for the United States under its Manifest Destiny doctrine. He massacred hundreds of indigenous people while exploring in Northern California, returning to Monterey, the capital of Alta California, and defeating the Mexican forces there and in Los Angeles during the Mexican-American War (1846–1848). The Treaty of Guadalupe Hidalgo on February 2, 1848, ended the war with Mexico and ceded Alta California and the Southwest to the United States. (Right, courtesy of the Library of Congress; below, courtesy of the Smithsonian Institution.)

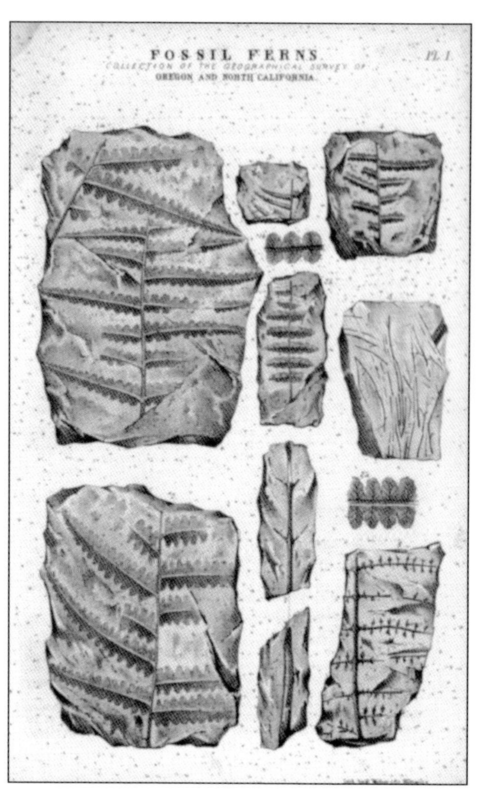

After John C. Fremont found fossils in California during his 1843 expedition, he sent them to James Hall, state geologist of New York, who identified them as ferns from the Triassic period. Together, they published two papers on them in 1845, the first about California fossils. (Courtesy of the Smithsonian Institution.)

At Mission San Juan Capistrano in California, fossiliferous rock 16.5 million years old (Miocene) was quarried by indigenous people to construct the mission (1776) and its church (1806). On October 10, 1812, an earthquake destroyed the church, and 40 people were killed by falling stones. The ruins still lie near where they fell in 1812. Fossils are present in these and in stones in other buildings. (Author's collection.)

A week before the Mexican-American War ended in 1848, gold was discovered at Sutter's Mill in the Sierra Nevada. Pres. James Polk announced the discovery to Congress on December 5, 1848, setting off the 1849 Gold Rush, hence the name forty-niners. Americans came west by horse and wagon or caught ships to California, while other people from around the world came to San Francisco and then to the goldfields. Gravels, filling ancient Eocene (45–48 mya) river valleys, were hydraulically mined (above) for gold, which exposed clay layers with abundant leaf fossils (at right is *Macginitiea whitneyi*). The Geological Survey of California (GSC) collected the fossils, but they were destroyed in a fire, so the GSC used C.D. Voy's fossils collected in the 1860s for its reports. (Above, courtesy of US Geological Survey; right, courtesy of UCMP.)

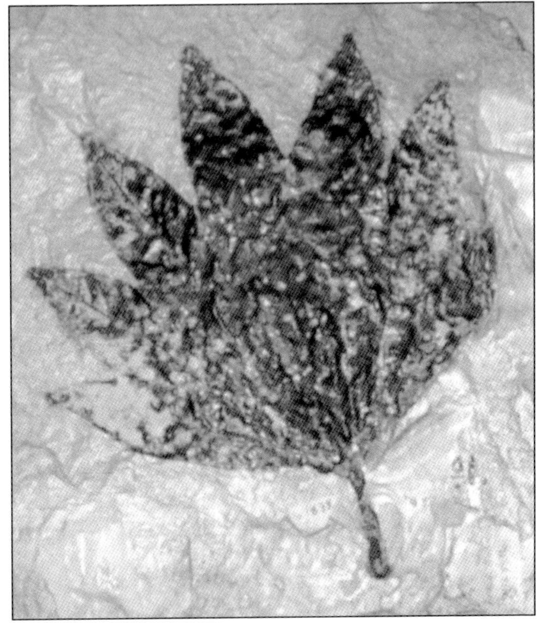

Congress declared California a state in 1850, but it had no flag. The Bear Flag Revolt in June 1846 against the Mexican garrison at Sonoma declared the California Republic. Although the republic did not last long, the state flag, adopted officially in 1911 (above), was based on that bear flag, both showing a California grizzly bear. The bear became a permanent symbol for California. The bear is extinct now; the last one was shot in 1922, making California the only state with an extinct animal on its flag and seal and designated as its state animal (1953). Grizzly bear fossils occur in Rancho La Brea and other ice age deposits along with perhaps two other species of bear. The skull below is from a cave deposit near Shasta Lake. (Above, author's collection; below, courtesy of UCMP.)

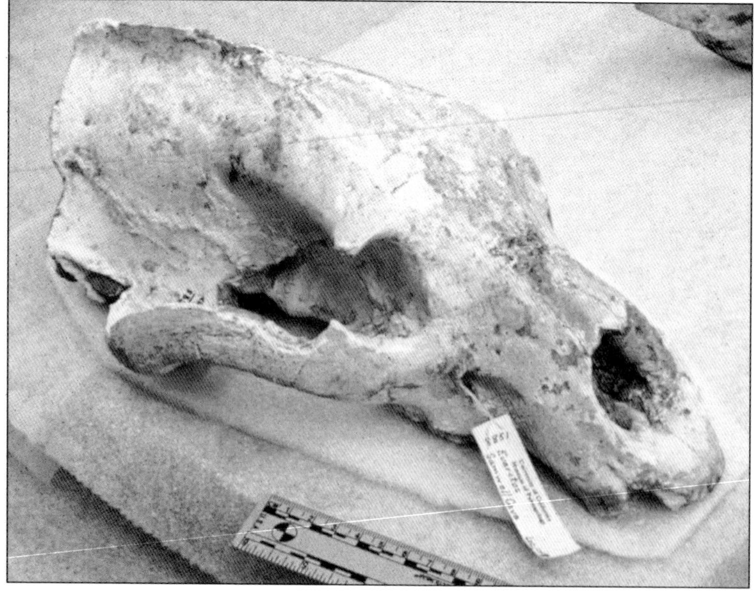

Initially, the California legislature contracted with J.B. Trask to survey the state in 1853 for mineral wealth. He produced a geologic map of the state. Later, Josiah D. Whitney (1819–1896, right), a geologist experienced in state geological surveys, was appointed state geologist and director of the GSC on April 26, 1860. His book *Metallic Wealth of the United States* (1854) likely influenced his appointment since California had such riches. Quickly organized, Whitney hired geologists and biologists. GSC field teams like the one below explored California, including its fossils, which now lie in the UCMP. Although the legislature was disappointed in Whitney's progress, the survey accomplished much in its 14 years—15 publications on paleontology and geology, maps, and books on Yosemite. Whitney later published another seven reports on geology and biology. (Both, courtesy of the Smithsonian Institution.)

The GSC (1860–1874) consisted of seven men in 1863. From left to right are C. Averill (accountant and field assistant), W.M. Gabb (paleontologist), W. Ashburner (field assistant), Josiah D. Whitney (state geologist), C.F. Hoffmann (topographer), C. King (field assistant and geologist), and W.H. Brewer (field leader). The legislature, expecting the GSC to focus on applied geology, was disappointed with the survey's report on paleontology and Whitney's complaints about insufficient funding and failure to find geologic riches. Whitney replied, "It is not the business of a geological surveying corps to act . . . as a prospecting party. We have escaped perils by flood and field, have evaded the friendly embrace of the grizzly, and now find ourselves in the jaws of the Legislature." With no budget in 1867, surveying in 1868 was terminated. The legislature ended the GSC in 1874, ordering Whitney to deposit its collections, including fossils, in the state university. Those fossils formed the basis for UCMP's collections. (Courtesy of the California State Library.)

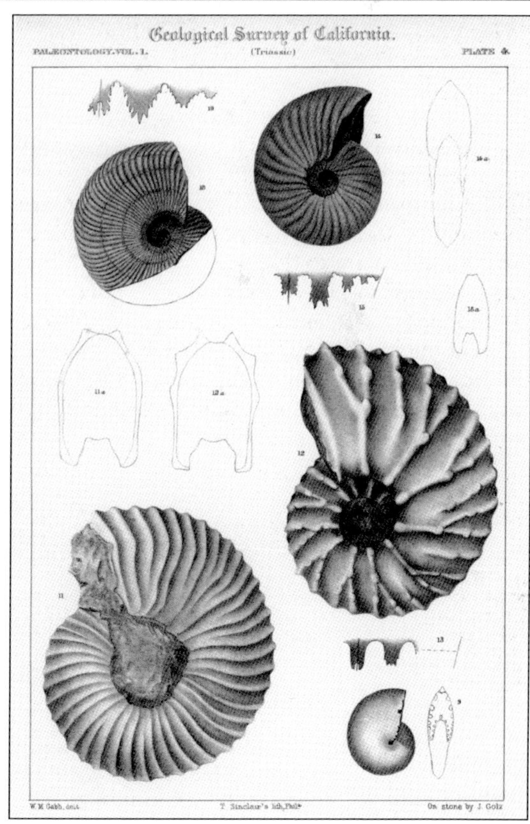

The GSC's *Palaeontology, Volume 1*, published in 1864, described fossils, many new to science. The volume, beautifully bound with an image of an ammonite (*Ammonites chicoensis* from plate 13, figure 17 in the book) embossed in gold on the front cover (above) and the GSC seal on the back cover, has four sections and a preface by Josiah Whitney. In its 241 pages and 32 lithographic plates, Carboniferous and Jurassic fossils are described by F.B. Meek and Triassic and Cretaceous fossils by W.M. Gabb. The legislature was disappointed with the book, as it did not focus on applied geology or resources. At right, plate 4 of GSC's *Palaeontology, Volume I* shows five fossils, including two newly named species, *Ceratites whitneyi* and *Ammonites blakei* to honor Whitney and W.P. Blake, who had previously studied California fossils. (Both, author's collection.)

Perhaps the most intriguing fossil locality is Alcatraz Island (above in 1895) in the San Francisco Bay. Famous for its prison and the movies made there, Alcatraz was explored by the GSC prior to 1864. Rocks and fossils of Cretaceous age were found, and two of the fossils collected are in the UCMP GSC collection: *Inoceramus elliotti* and *Lucina alcatrazis* (below). These fossils were restudied by F. Anderson in 1938 when he named the species of *Lucina* for the island. The same rocks are exposed throughout the Bay Area along with a mixture of older rocks that have been crushed by tectonic processes so that fossils are rare except in special geologic circumstances. Alcatraz is now a popular tourist spot. (Above, courtesy of National Park Service; below, courtesy of Dave Strauss, www.dscomposition.com.)

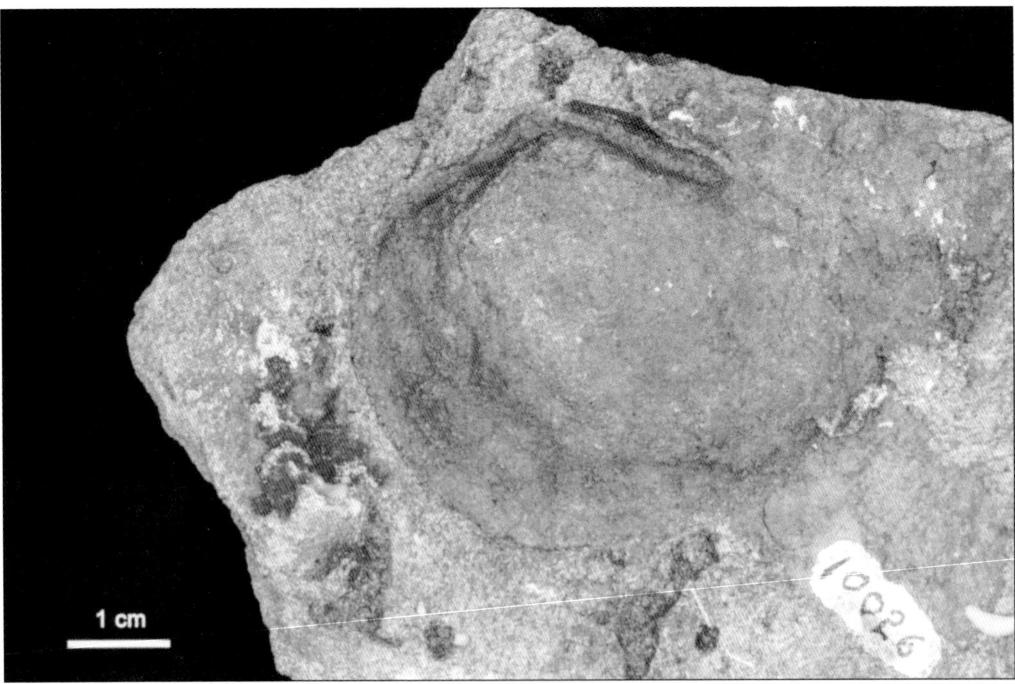

Two

Building Paleontology

The University of California did not exist until 1868. The Morrill Act, signed by Abraham Lincoln in 1862, provided for grants of federal lands to the states to build so-called Land Grant Colleges. With that, the state legislature established the university through an agreement with the College of California in Oakland to merge with it and to buy its lands in present-day Berkeley. The land occupation had progressed from the ancestral lands of the indigenous Ohlone people prior to 1797, to Mission San Jose in 1797, a land grant for the Spaniard Luís María Peralta in 1820, Mexico in 1821, the United States in 1848, California in 1850, the College of California in 1853, and finally, the University of California in 1868.

Faculty was hired in 1868, and classes opened in 1869 at the college in Oakland. John and Joseph LeConte were among the first 10 faculty members at UC, with John teaching physics and Joseph teaching geology, natural history, and botany. Born on a rice plantation in Georgia, the LeConte brothers held positions at the University of Georgia and South Carolina College (precursor to today's University of South Carolina) where they had earned the respect and honors of the American scientific community. After the Civil War, they decided to leave the South and find positions elsewhere. Joseph had broad interests in science, including paleontology, and taught undergraduate students who admired him. Although Joseph published and lectured extensively on a variety of scientific topics, unfortunately he held negative views of black people and of women that are not acceptable now. As a result, his name has been removed from buildings, sites, and objects named for him.

The creation of a university for California had been discussed seriously before statehood but the resources to build it did not exist, in spite of a 53,000-acre grant of federal land in 1853. In Oakland, California, Rev. Henry Durant and Dr. Samuel H. Willey founded the Contra Costa Academy (1853) to provide a liberal arts education to boys. They renamed it the College of California in 1855. By the 1860s, it was cash poor but land rich. The State of California agreed to transition from the College of California to the newly authorized University of California, and purchased for it the college's land four miles from Oakland. The legislature passed the Organic Act on March 23, 1868, establishing the university and a board of regents to run it, and specifying a list of colleges to be included. The university opened at the College of California location in downtown Oakland to 42 students and a faculty of 10, including the brothers John and Joseph LeConte, on September 23, 1869. (Courtesy of the J. Paul Getty Museum.)

The College of California covered four square blocks in downtown Oakland. Faculty and students lived nearby until the new UC campus opened in 1873 on land that would become UC Berkeley. Joseph and John LeConte lived close to the college on Twelfth Street (shown above in 1870) and traveled to Berkeley by horse car (below) in 1873 and 1874. (Above, courtesy of Stanford Library; below, courtesy of the Oakland Public Library.)

The Morrill Act, signed into federal law by Abraham Lincoln in 1862, established public, so-called land grant, state universities. California received 150,000 acres of public land, the sale of which provided funds to establish and build the University of California. A bronze bust near the base of UC's campanile (on the south side) honors Lincoln. It is a replica, installed on February 12, 1921, of a 1908 marble bust by Gutzon de la Mothe Borglum, who sculpted the presidents at Mount Rushmore. Former Berkeley student and owner of the *Washington Post* Eugene Meyer gave the original marble bust to the US Congress in 1908. It stands 40 inches (100 cm) high and weighs about 375 pounds (170 kilograms). Meyer donated replicas in 1909 to the University of California, the White House, and several other organizations. (Both, author's collection.)

Just as the new university was organizing, a major earthquake occurred on the Hayward Fault on October 10, 1868 (estimated magnitude of 6.3–6.7). It impacted the 260,000 East Bay residents, killing 30 and damaging structures like Mission San José (pictured) built in 1797, the Peralta home built in 1840, and the Alameda County Courthouse, constructed in 1857 in San Leandro. The College of California in central Oakland was shaken badly, with people pouring into the streets and horses running amok. The university could still function when it opened in 1869 at the college's location. The fault has a long history of large earthquakes. It passes through the UC campus and is expected to produce similar large earthquakes in the future. Because of it and the San Andreas Fault west of San Francisco, earthquakes are a major concern. UC Berkeley took precautions for earthquakes by retrofitting its structures and developing evacuation procedures. UCMP guards its collections with special padding, containers, and cabinets; the *Tyrannosaurus rex* rolls on its platform. (Courtesy of Library of Congress.)

John (1818–1891) and Joseph LeConte (1823–1901) were born at Woodmanston, a 3,354-acre rice plantation in the lowlands of Liberty County, Georgia, established by their granduncle William LeConte and grandfather John Eatton LeConte in 1769. Their father, Louis, born there in 1782, later assumed its management. The plantation had 231 enslaved people. John and Joseph explored the swamps, forests, and their father's famous botanical garden, developing a passion for science. Joseph is shown here holding a quartz crystal in his hand with several others on a table beside him in a 1944 painting by Kate Flournoy Edwards. It hangs in the lobby of LeConte Hall, home to the history department at the University of Georgia. Joseph LeConte was notable for his pursuit of geology, hence the crystals in the portrait. (Author's collection.)

John and Joseph LeConte lived on Woodmanston Plantation until age 15 when they started college at the University of Georgia; first John in 1833, then Joseph five years later in 1838. Just as Joseph entered college, their father died. The brothers and a sister inherited portions of Woodmanston; Joseph received 484 acres and 40 slaves. John decided not to return to his property, leaving it to be managed by his sister, while Joseph, who at 15 could not hold title to property, decided when he became owner that he would put it under an overseer, returning every year to check on it. By 1860, the US Census reported that Joseph LeConte owned 63 slaves, 21 younger than 10 and 4 older than 50. The enslaved people, besides tending the plantation, did everything necessary for the daily life of the LeConte family. Their numerous descendants took the name LeCounte and now work to preserve the history of their ancestors and the plantation. In 2003, they restored the slave cabin shown here. They hold a reunion at LeConte-Woodmanston Plantation every two years. (Author's collection.)

The LeConte family worshipped at Midway Congregational Church most Sundays. They traveled the eight miles from Woodmanston Plantation by horse and buggy. The original meetinghouse, built in 1756, was burned by the British in the Revolutionary War. The church pictured here was built in 1792. Like most churches in the South, both white members and their slaves attended services. Its cemetery is across Highway 17 from the church. (Author's collection.)

Joseph LeConte's father, mother, and other ancestors are interred in the plot shown here in the Midway Cemetery. His father, Louis, was religious and passed that on to Joseph, who became even more devoted when his father died in 1835. Joseph relished the mountains and land as God's creations, especially exemplified by Yosemite Valley, and believed evolution was directed by God. In Berkeley, Joseph helped found four churches. (Author's collection.)

Before the Civil War, the LeContes taught at South Carolina College in Columbia. Gen. W.T. Sherman, in his March to the Sea from Atlanta in December 1864 (right), swept through Georgia with raiders who foraged off the land. They destroyed Woodmanston as they pushed on to Charleston and Columbia. The troops burned Columbia but not South Carolina College. From December 9, 1864, to February 24, 1865, Joseph LeConte struggled through Sherman's troops to Woodmanston to check on his slaves and property. There, LeConte offered his enslaved people the choice of staying, going with him to Columbia, or going where they wished as free people. Most stayed on the plantation. Before LeConte returned, his wife and two daughters watched Columbia burn (below) on February 17 from their house on campus, the Third Professors House (now Lieber College). (Both, courtesy of the Library of Congress.)

HARPER'S WEEKLY. 217

April 8, 1865.]

THE BURNING OF COLUMBIA, SOUTH CAROLINA, February 17, 1865.—[Sketched by W. Waud.]

UNIVERSITY OF SOUTH CAROLINA.

EXAMINATION IN GEOLOGY, - - - JUNE, 1869.

PROFESSOR JOSEPH LeCONTE.

1. State the conditions under which *Deltas* and *Estuaries* are generally formed, and *how*, in each case. Give the evidences of gradual subsidence in great deltas. 7
2. Give the formula for determining the depth of an earthquake shock when the velocity of the spherical wave and the velocity of the surface wave is known, and show how the formula is obtained. 10
3. Give Darwin's theory of the formation of barrier and of atoll reefs, and the proofs of its truth. 9
4. Show how *fossils* are used to determine *contemporaneousness* of strata. Give the general *principle* of the determination. State the *limitations* of the principle and apply to the *older* and to the *newer* strata. 10
5. Give the mode of origin and the general structure of mountain chains. Give the two kinds of mountains and the characteristics of each and illustrate. 8
6. Prove that auriferous quartz veins have been filled by deposit from *hot alkaline solutions*. 11
7. Give the most probable theory as to the conditions under which a *coal basin* was formed, and apply to our own coal fields. 11
8. In what strata are salt deposits found? Give examples? Compare salt with coal as to its mode of occurrence. Give the most probable theory of the formation of a *salt basin*. 9
9. Define *synthetic or connecting types*. Give examples from each great division of the earth's history. 7

After the war, the LeContes became so distraught with the state legislature and college, they searched for jobs elsewhere. The LeContes were major figures in American science, and with recommendations from Eastern scientists, they were offered positions at the new University of California for fall 1869. Joseph taught at South Carolina until June 1869, giving a final exam in geology (left, first page only), and then traveled to California. The University of South Carolina named LeConte College in 1910 to honor the brothers, which was replaced by a newly constructed college of the same name in 1952 (below). (Left, courtesy of University of South Carolina; below, author's collection.)

Joseph LeConte and John Muir (right) shared common interests in Yosemite and the Sierra Nevada. On a field trip in 1870 after arriving in California, LeConte and his party met John Muir in Yosemite Valley (above) in August. They discussed the origin of the valley, concluding it was carved by glaciers during a recent ice age, which was in contrast to Josiah Whitney, who believed the valley formed as the earth cracked open. LeConte's group and Muir left the valley, passing Tanaya Lake and Mono Pass on the way to Mono Lake. Muir left them there; LeConte went north to Lake Tahoe. In 1890, LeConte and Muir met to discuss the founding of the Sierra Club. Muir was first president of the club from 1892 to 1914. Joseph LeConte served on the board of directors from 1892 to 1898. (Above, author's collection; right, courtesy of Smithsonian Institution.)

South Hall, the first building constructed at UC (1873), housed a lecture hall holding 500 students, laboratories, offices, and administration. Joseph LeConte taught here until 1896. In 1905, it caught fire due to an electrical short near paleontology professor John Merriam's lab. Richard Rowe, a janitor, and Eustace Furlong, a paleontology student, attacked the fire with water buckets placed in the hall for such emergencies. This building still stands at UC. (Author's collection.)

The Museum of Natural Sciences, supervised by Joseph LeConte, contained fossils and other items on the first floor of South Hall. The building at the time of the fire was worth about $50,000, but the fossils acquired by LeConte and Merriam were irreplaceable. The paleontology collection survived and remained in South Hall from 1873 to 1911 with parts of it stored in other buildings. (Courtesy of UCMP Archives.)

Joseph LeConte lectured in South Hall (right) throughout his career at UC. He was recognized as a popular, versatile, and outstanding professor responsible for developing strong curricula and enhancing the reputation of the university with his research and writing. Indeed, LeConte was offered positions at the Universities of Georgia, South Carolina, and Virginia but stayed in California. LeConte's first classes in 1869 kept growing in size until they numbered 450 students in the 1880s, too many for him as he aged. At 68, he relinquished his classes to John Merriam, his student and now a professor himself. LeConte and his wife, Caroline (below), lived near the campus and enjoyed visits from students and colleagues. (Both, courtesy of UCMP Archives.)

Bird's-eye View of Marble Cañon from the Vermilion Cliffs, near the Mouth of the Paria. In the distance the Colorado River is seen to turn to the west, where its gorge divides the Twin Plateaus. On the right are seen the Eastern Karbab Displacements appearing as folds, and farther in the distance as faults.

ELEMENTS

OF

GEOLOGY:

A TEXT-BOOK

FOR

COLLEGES AND FOR THE GENERAL READER.

BY

JOSEPH LE CONTE,

AUTHOR OF "RELIGION AND SCIENCE," ETC., AND PROFESSOR OF GEOLOGY AND NATURAL HISTORY IN THE UNIVERSITY OF CALIFORNIA.

NEW YORK:
D. APPLETON AND COMPANY,
549 AND 551 BROADWAY.
1878.

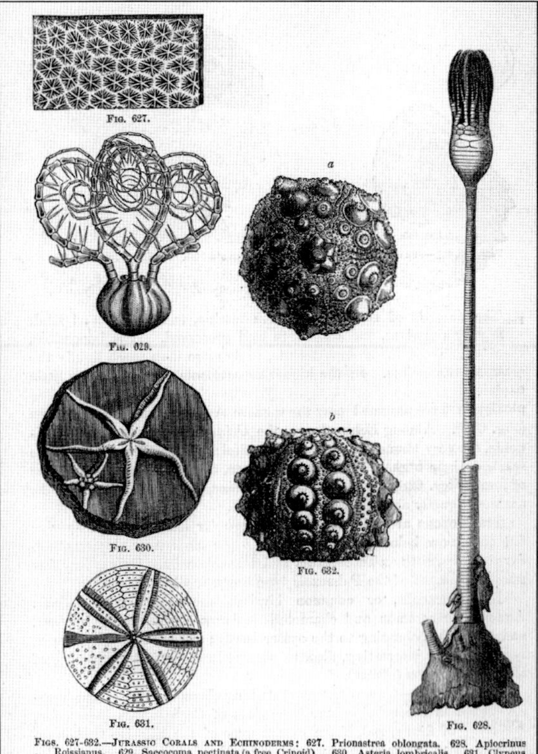

Figs. 627-632.—Jurassic Corals and Echinoderms: 627. Prionastrea oblongata. 628. Apiocrinus Roissianus. 629. Saccocoma pectinata (a free Crinoid). 630. Asteria lombricalis. 631. Clypeus Plotii. 632. *a b*, Hemicidaris crenularis.

Joseph LeConte's energy and interests benefitted paleontology, but he only did research on Pleistocene ground sloth footprints uncovered by prisoners in the state prison yard in Carson, Nevada. Recognizing that past life was critically important to Earth's and life's history, he acquired fossils for the museum and his lectures: Whitfield's fossils from the eastern United States and Europe for $6,290 (1886); Bassett's crinoids from Crawfordsville, Indiana, for $1,000 (1886); Stern's shell collection for $1,500 (1887); and the donated Pioche and Voy collections. His textbook *Elements of Geology* (1878, five editions) and his books *Compend of Geology* (1888) and *Evolution and its Relation to Religious Thought* (1880) contain illustrations of fossils. The *Elements of Geology* is richly illustrated with over 900 figures, about half of which show fossils. Clearly, LeConte knew paleontology and relied on it in his writings and lectures. (Both, author's collection.)

Joseph LeConte (right) was held in high esteem for his writing and lectures on geology, evolution, vision, and other topics. Below, a stereograph describes him as a "great scientist." Elected president of the American Association for the Advancement of Science, the Geological Society of America, and a member of the National Academy of Sciences, he was also called "The Prince of Evolutionists" in 1897 and "The Gentle Prophet of Evolution." He was honored by the naming of the following places and features: the LeConte Lodges in Yosemite and Great Smoky Mountains; university buildings at Berkeley, Georgia, and South Carolina; schools in Berkeley and Los Angeles; and sites like mountains in California and Tennessee; cascades and rapids in the Sierras; streets in Berkeley, Los Angeles, and Athens; and sequoia trees in the Sierras and oak trees at UC Berkeley. (Both, courtesy of UCMP Archives.)

The former LeConte Hall at UC (1923–2020), designed by famed architect John Galen Howard, was named for John LeConte, professor of physics, interim president (1869), and president (1874–1881). Joseph's name was added later when the building was designated a national historic place in 1928. Joseph LeConte not only once owned 63 slaves and provided services to the Confederate army as a contractor for the Nitre and Mining Corps at pay equal to a major in that Army, but he also maintained that black people were inferior to white people and that they needed supervision and the help of the white race. His paternalistic and racist views are reprehensible and certainly not acceptable today. In November 2020, Chancellor Carol Christ stated: "His words and deeds profoundly conflict with our values, and with our commitment to equity, inclusion and a true sense of belonging for every member of our community." Thus, LeConte Hall was unnamed in 2020. Other structures, like a Berkeley public school and the Sierra Club lodge in Yosemite, were renamed. (Author's collection.)

Joseph LeConte's 1901 visit to Yosemite Valley (shown here in 1887), where he had gone many times since 1870, began in June with his daughter Sallie and members of the Sierra Club. It was his final visit. On July 6, Joseph LeConte, with Sallie by his side, died in his tent on the floor of the valley he loved. (Courtesy of UCMP Archives.)

Joseph LeConte's friends placed his body in a wooden box, took it by coach to a train, and then to San Francisco. He was buried at Mountain View Cemetery in Oakland in a grave marked by a slab of granite from Yosemite. His death was reported widely in the local Bay Area newspapers, and more places were named for him, including the Sierra Club lodge in Yosemite Valley in 1904. (Author's collection.)

Women were not admitted to UC in 1869 as was common in American higher education. However, the regents and 10-man faculty debated whether or not to admit them. Joseph LeConte initially spoke against women, suggesting they would "swarm" the university, but later relented, saying that educated women would be better mothers and homemakers, a view he long held. Thus, in 1870, a total of 12 women were admitted in the second UC class; three years later, 222 women and 167 men were enrolled at UC. By 1900, nearly 60 percent of the 2,906 students were women, and they graduated with men, seen here on May 15, 1901. The first woman and second student to graduate in paleontology, Edna Wemple completed her master of science degree in 1907. Women remained few in paleontology early on but increased in student, faculty, and staff numbers. Of over 425 paleontology dissertations since 1904, women earned 110 of them. Perhaps the most influential person in UCMP's history was Annie Alexander, benefactress, collector, and expedition organizer from 1900 to 1950. (Courtesy of Bancroft Library.)

Three

A Paleontology Program Emerges

Joseph LeConte's best student, John C. Merriam, came to UC because he read LeConte's textbook *Elements of Geology*. Merriam finished his bachelor's degree and went to Munich to study under famed paleontologist Karl von Zittel for his doctorate. He returned to UC in 1894 as the first paleontologist in the new geology department. Merriam immediately began a teaching and research program in paleontology and soon acquired a number of students. Annie Alexander audited Merriam's 1900 class and became interested in the subject. A wealthy woman, she became an ardent proponent and financial supporter of paleontology at UC and a believer in a museum to house the fossils. In 1912, Merriam was appointed chairman of the Department of Paleontology, formed in 1909. He was appointed dean of the faculties in 1920 but also was appointed president of the Carnegie Institute of Washington. Annie Alexander negotiated to establish and endow a Museum of Paleontology as a separate research unit. In the meantime, other paleontologists had been hired as faculty or instructors. In 1915, seven faculty and instructors taught in the department. With the help of Annie Alexander, UCMP was finally established in 1921. The Department of Paleontology was the only such department in America until 1989, when it merged with other biology departments to form a single, larger Department of Integrative Biology. Paleontology grew as a discipline on campus and in the United States, but this growth was stopped by World War II in 1941.

John C. Merriam (1869–1945) was appointed instructor of paleontology in the geology department when he returned from Munich in 1894. He offered the first course in general paleontology in 1894–1895 and took over LeConte's class in 1896. Interest in paleontology by students grew so that by 1897–1898, Merriam taught eight courses in paleontology and historical geology. His lectures were well regarded, his research accomplished, and his expeditions outstanding. Students such as Loye Holmes Miller, Chester Stock, and Edna Wemple gladly took his classes. He began research on Tertiary invertebrates but switched to vertebrates of Triassic marine reptiles in Shasta County, Tertiary vertebrates at John Day in Oregon, and fossil mammals in the San Francisco Bay region. He would later organize expeditions to collect fossils in these regions and elsewhere, like Rancho La Brea in Los Angeles and the Triassic beds of Nevada. Shown here in 1905, Merriam photographs the geology of the Triassic beds in Nevada. The shell mounds built by the indigenous Ohlone people fascinated him, and in 1902, he began excavations of the Emeryville shell mound. (Courtesy of UCMP Archives.)

John C. Merriam organized an expedition in 1899 to the John Day fossil beds in Oregon with several others (above, campsite), traveling by ship, train, and horse. It was supported financially by J.B. Reinstein, a regent of UC, as arranged by "Doc Joe" as the students called Joseph LeConte. The fossils were abundant. At right, Merriam (left) and Loye Holmes Miller are shown collecting the fossils that were brought to the campus for study by Merriam and his students. This expedition started a longstanding interest in John Day paleontology by UC paleontologists that continues today. Merriam believed the fossil beds and the unique geology around them should be made a park. In 1974, the John Day National Monument was established with a visitor center and facilities to study the fossils. (Both, courtesy of UCMP Archives.)

Annie Alexander (1867–1950) audited John Merriam's paleontology class in 1900, beginning her long interest in the subject. She was born in Honolulu to Samuel and Martha Cooke. In 1869, Samuel partnered with Henry Baldwin to purchase 12 acres on Maui to grow sugar cane. Sugar cane plantations were tended by people brought from Asia to work in the fields for a few dollars a month. The work was hard, but the sugar grew well, and Alexander and Baldwin profited handsomely. The corporation became successful and still exists. In 1886, the family moved to Oakland. Annie eventually ended up in Merriam's 1900 class. Here, she is shown in the field with her brother's shotgun. (Courtesy of UCMP Archives.)

Annie Alexander and John Merriam brought back fossils that had to be prepared so they could be studied as shown in these two c. 1902 photographs of early preparation labs in South Hall. Prep labs are equipped to remove rock from the fossils with hand tools like hammers, chisels, probes, and picks; use liquids to free small fossils; soak samples in acids to dissolve the rock; and just use people power. Puzzle solving and special glue are used to restore broken skulls, bones, and shells. The fossils from Rancho La Brea and McKittrick embedded in tar-soaked sand are particularly difficult and messy to extract. Every fossil is a new preparation problem. Over time, power tools and other innovations were introduced, making the work easier. Nevertheless, a large skeleton could take years to prepare for study. (Both, courtesy of UCMP Archives.)

With Merriam's encouragement, Annie Alexander mounted her own expedition in 1901 to Fossil Lake, Oregon, a dry lake bed with Pleistocene fossils exposed on its surface and sediments. Arriving in June, Alexander's group included Herbert W.F. Furlong, a 29-year-old student and preparator for Merriam; William B. Greeley, a 21-year-old student; Mary E. Wilson, a teacher and friend; an African American wagon driver and cook; and a 14-year-old boy. Along the way, Alexander posed with her brother's shotgun (page 42). At Fossil Lake, they recovered 300 pounds of fossils in five days, mostly of the extinct horse *Hipparion*, but also camels, elephants, rodents, and birds. In April 2009 (below), students from UCMP visited Fossil Lake to track Alexander's expedition, but snow made collecting difficult, and only a few bones were found. (Above, courtesy of UCMP Archives; below, author's collection.)

California has a bounty of oil. Tar from seeps was first used by indigenous people to seal boats and fix broken things, and as medicine. The first California oil well was drilled in 1865, followed by 3,000 more by 1899. Only three fields were major producers—McKittrick (1899, above), Kern River (1899), and Brea Canyon (1899)—which together with previous wells, like at Taft (below in 1902), amounted to two million barrels a year. Little demand existed then, although that changed after 1900 when exploration increased worldwide. Paleontology was used to date, correlate, and evaluate strata being drilled. With microscopic and abundant foraminifera, micropaleontology became essential by 1921 in exploration and development of oil fields. UC provided students and research on foraminifera through the 1980s, when geophysical methods did much the same tasks. (Both, courtesy of UCMP.)

From 1905 to 1907 and 1912 to 1913, John Merriam collected at Rancho La Brea in Los Angeles with students. Owner George Hancock then gave Los Angeles County excavation rights and in 1924 also gave 23 acres for Hancock Park to preserve and exhibit the fossils. UC groups collected thousands of bones dating from 50,000 to 10,000 years ago. The fossil species are widespread from Alaska to Central America. (Courtesy of UCMP Archives.)

The George C. Page Museum opened in 1974 with exhibits of articulated skeletons. An open pit showing bones in the tar, other seeps, and statues of reconstructed animals also adorn the grounds. The fossils characterize the Rancholabrean time from 250,000 to 12,000 years ago. A former asphalt quarry, now a lake, has mammoth models on rafts and along the shoreline. John Merriam's interpretations provide the basis for some exhibits. (Author's collection.)

The Rancho La Brea collection caused an immediate storage problem for the tons of material. The iconic campanile (Sather Tower) was under construction from 1913 to 1914. The fossils were stored there even before it was finished. The campanile has tall floors filled with La Brea and, later, McKittrick tar seep fossils. They are still there after almost 110 years and are being actively studied by UCMP paleontologists. (Author's collection.)

This room contains fossils from McKittrick tar seeps, while La Brea material is kept in other rooms of the campanile. Visiting scholar William Pannapacker inspects a McKittrick fossil room as part of his interests in museum facilities and functions. Another floor houses the carillonneur who plays the tower's bells. (Author's collection.)

John C. Merriam sent several expeditions from 1901 to 1903 to the Shasta region of northeastern California to collect Triassic vertebrates. They were financed and overseen by Annie Alexander. Participants took trains to Redding and then continued on horses to the fossiliferous outcrops. The expedition is seen here while on the 1902 trip. The horses are loaded with camping gear, rations, collecting equipment, and fossils. (Courtesy of UCMP Archives.)

Fossil collecting at Shasta varied from excellent to poor, depending on rock type. Each fossil was removed by carefully excavating around the bones, protecting them with a plaster jacket, and then taking them to the university for preparation and study. Faculty and students described their finds in scientific papers, often in the *University of California Publications in Geological Sciences*. Stanford faculty collaborated in fieldwork. (Courtesy of UCMP Archives.)

John Merriam and Annie Alexander led and financed an expedition in May and June 1905 to collect fossil reptiles in the Humboldt Mountains of Nevada. The Saurian Expedition consisted of two women and five men. Alexander wrote, "For two days I watched with fascinated eyes the work of excavation," as ichthyosaurs (huge marine lizards) were removed from Triassic limestones. "Little by little the blocks were marked and wrapped and packed down to camp on the backs of our horses," she wrote. (Both, courtesy of UCMP Archives.)

John Merriam, Annie Alexander, and Edna Mary Wemple are eating lunch among limestone blocks. About meals, Alexander remarked: "Night after night we stood before a hot fire to stir rice, or beans, or corn, or soup, contriving the best dinners we could out of our dwindling supply of provisions. We sometimes wondered if the men thought the firewood dropped out of the sky or whether a fairy godmother brought it to our door, for they never asked any questions." Nevertheless, both women enjoyed collecting fossils and filling the wagon with them. (Both, courtesy of UCMP Archives.)

Students of John Merriam worked on many different topics. Edna Mary Wemple is shown here on the 1905 Saurian Expedition leaning against an outcrop of limestone. The first woman and second paleontology student, she earned a master of arts degree in 1907. Her thesis on Triassic shark teeth collected on the Saurian Expedition was three pages long but dealt with the teeth authoritatively, even describing new species. She later became a teacher. (Courtesy of UCMP Archives.)

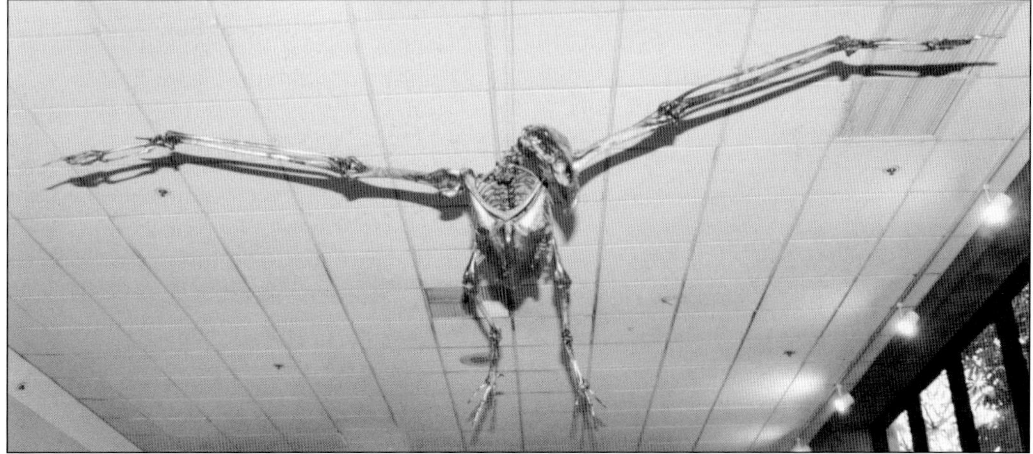

Loye Holmes Miller (1874–1970) studied fossil birds from Rancho La Brea with John Merriam for his doctorate degree in 1912. In 1909, he described *Teratornis merriami* (which hangs in the Page Museum at La Brea). Its wingspan was 11–12 feet, the wing area 188 square feet, and its estimated weight was 50 pounds. Miller became professor at UC's Southern Branch, later known as University of California, Los Angeles (UCLA). He founded its zoology department, staying there until the mid-1960s. (Author's collection.)

Annie Alexander supported paleontology but did not like the collections being in the Department of Geology. Paleontology has traditionally been part of geology departments. It depends on geology for understanding the ages and environments of the fossils and their relationships to other fossils found elsewhere, as seen in the geology at Red Rock Canyon State Park, California. There, fossiliferous beds, Miocene 12 to 8 mya, are tilted and have internal structures that bear on fossil occurrences. The beds have yielded, among other things, horse, camel, antelope, saber-toothed cats, bone-crushing dogs, and plants. However, paleontology also requires an understanding of anatomy and the biology of fossils. Thus, vertebrate paleontology is commonly taught in biology. Alexander, however, thought paleontology should have its own department to alleviate strains in the geology department. In 1909, a Department of Paleontology was formed with John Merriam in charge. The new department was housed in South Hall, but Alexander negotiated with the president to get new quarters in Bacon Hall in 1911 for geology, paleontology, and the fossil collection. (Author's collection.)

The Bacon Art and Library Building (1881–1930), like South Hall, was on the central campus. It housed the library and the newly acquired art collection. It had a three-story rotunda with two upper galleries that overlooked a central open area. The library in 1881 held over 17,000 volumes. In 1908, the collection had grown to 160,000 volumes, and the building was seriously crowded. In 1911, the library moved to the new Doe Library, the building was renovated and renamed Bacon Hall, and the paleontology collections and paleontologists moved into it. Fossil exhibits and the fossil collections were arranged around the rotunda and remained there until they were moved again, this time to the Hearst Memorial Mining Building in 1931. (Courtesy of UCMP Archives.)

This photograph shows the buildings on the Berkeley campus in 1906. The great San Francisco earthquake of April 1906 badly damaged the buildings. From right to left are South Hall (opened 1873), Bacon Hall (1881), Mining and Mechanical Arts Building (1879), and North Hall (1873). All but South Hall were eventually razed. The fossil collection in South Hall was not damaged by the earthquake, but the possibility of another earthquake was worrisome. Indeed, the Loma Prieta

earthquake of 1989 on the San Andreas Fault near Santa Cruz shook the campus and UCMP, causing books in the library to fall and fossils in UCMP to rattle around in the Earth Science Building. All buildings on campus are seismically retrofitted, and the UCMP fossils protected. (Courtesy of UCMP Archives.)

As Annie Alexander was planning to collect in Alaska in 1908, she met Louise Kellogg and invited her along; from this, a lifelong relationship developed. Three years later, they bought 525 acres on Grizzly Island in the Sacramento–San Joaquin River Delta. For several years, they camped on the land while trying to grow crops and livestock. Crops were difficult to grow at times, especially when the tides brought seawater into the delta. However, their cattle won prizes for their quality. The women slowly constructed farm buildings and eventually a 30-by-30-foot house for themselves. During this time, they also continued trips to collect mammals, fossils, and plants from places in the West and Mexico. They still organized expeditions with paleontologists and collecting trips of their own. This recent photograph shows the fields of their ranch, but all the buildings were removed long ago by new owners. The land is now part of the Grizzly Island Wildlife Area of California. (Author's collection.)

The Department of Paleontology faculty and instructors had grown to seven by 1915. From left to right are (first row) J.P. Buwalda, J.C. Merriam, C. Stock, and B.L. Clark; (second row) E.L. Packard, W.S.W. Kew, and J.O. Nomland. Only Merriam was a professor then, but Buwalda, Clark, and Stock became professors later. Annie Alexander continued to collect fossils for the department, and by 1915, the collection numbered over 150,000 invertebrate specimens, 15,000 vertebrates, and 3,000 plants, more than any museum west of the Mississippi River. The California Academy had a more extensive collection of fossils, but they were lost when the academy was completely destroyed in the Great San Francisco earthquake and fire of 1906. UCMP's collection became the primary one in California. (Courtesy of UCMP Archives.)

From 1921 to 1927, John Merriam excavated the McKittrick tar seep, one of 100 known in California, in the western San Joaquin Valley; those fossils are now in the campanile. The 9,000–13,000-year-old fossils, Rancholabrean in age, include dire wolves, coyotes, camels, mammoths, birds, wood, seeds, and diverse insects. The UCMP's McKittrick and La Brea collections of ice age animals are among the largest in the world. (Courtesy of UCMP Archives.)

A 2003 view of the McKittrick tar seeps shows the road passing through the tar, which pools in low spots where water also accumulates. Fossils are fairly abundant in places. Tar seeps occur on both sides of the road and still capture modern mammals, birds, and lots of water beetles in the sticky tar. (Author's collection.)

The Museum of Paleontology was officially established as a separate research unit of the University of California in 1921. Annie Alexander once again negotiated acquiring a museum for "her" fossils. She had long thought about it but was worried that the association of paleontology with geology would cause difficulties, so she held off. This was done to enhance John Merriam's role in paleontology, but he left for the Carnegie Institution that same year, greatly disappointing Alexander. UCMP, although independent, was always associated physically and administratively with the Department of Paleontology. It was the University of California Museum of Paleontology because Berkeley was the only UC campus in 1921. When the department moved out of the Hearst Memorial Mining Building in 1960, a student salvaged its sign and in 1998 returned it to the author, who was at that time the UCMP director. (Courtesy of UCMP Archives.)

Bruce L. Clark (1880–1945) was the first director of the UCMP from 1921 to 1926. He was appointed after John C. Merriam had moved to become president of the Carnegie Institution of Washington. The UCMP had just been authorized by the president of the university after negotiations with Annie Alexander. Clark's interest was invertebrate paleontology, but he became involved in field geology and increasing the collections by donations from oil companies from the California Coast Ranges, South America, and the East Indies. He also studied fossil radiolarians, publishing several papers on Cretaceous, Eocene, Oligocene, and Miocene forms with A.S. Campbell, a student of C. Kofoid's in the zoology department. Clark was an excellent teacher and supervised many graduate students. His most famous student was Esther Richards (later Applin), who worked on fossil snails with him. Clark resigned the directorship due to continuing interference in the UCMP by Merriam in Washington, DC. This began a turbulent time in paleontology at Berkeley. (Courtesy of UCMP.)

Pictured here in 1920 is Ester English Richards (1895–1972), the second woman to earn a master of arts paleontology degree at Berkeley (1920) on fossil snails with Professor Clark. In 1919, E.T. Dumble, Rio Bravo Oil Company, asked Clark to "recommend a man for a paleontology job." Clark asked, "I don't have a man, will a woman do?" She would indeed do and was hired to use larger fossils in oil exploration. With paleontologists Alva Ellisor and Hedwig Kniker in two other oil companies, she advocated using microscopic foraminifera instead. Richards proposed it at the 1921 Geological Society of America meeting. Afterwards, a Columbia University professor lamented, "Gentlemen, here is this chit of a girl right out of college, telling us we can use foraminifera to determine the age of formation. Gentlemen, you know it can't be done." However, she was right. It was the first major breakthrough in petroleum exploration. Three years later, over 300 micropaleontology jobs had been created and 31 micropaleontology courses begun at universities, perhaps the biggest applied impact ever by a Berkeley paleontology graduate. (Courtesy of Patty Kellogg.)

J.C. Merriam, seen in this portrait by Peter Van Valkenburgh (1870–1955) in 1932 when Merriam was in Washington, DC, did not want anything to do with the new museum. He insisted that Ralph Chaney, a paleobotanist, be appointed as chairman of the Department of Paleontology, leading to so much rancor that paleontology again became part of geology. Chaney was later appointed director of UCMP, but Annie Alexander objected so much to this that she withdrew her support to the museum. The university recanted its offer to Chaney and in 1927 appointed W.D. Matthew as director of UCMP and chairman of the reestablished Department of Paleontology. (Courtesy of UCMP Archives.)

William Diller Matthew (1871–1930) received his doctorate from Columbia University in 1895 studying vertebrate paleontology with the famous Henry Fairfield Osborn. He began his career at the American Museum of Natural History in New York City, where he worked between 1922 and 1927. UC offered him a professorship, chair of the Department of Paleontology, and directorship of the Museum of Paleontology in 1927. He was a highly regarded vertebrate paleontologist, publishing 240 scientific papers. Also in 1927, Matthew was elected to the Royal Society of London. He taught a popular introductory course in paleontology that reached the highest enrollment yet attained for a course of this kind. Courses on mammalian and avian paleontology were taken by graduate students, among them Hildegarde Howard (doctorate in zoology, 1928), who studied birds of La Brea and was later chief curator at the Los Angeles Natural History Museum, and Ruben A. Stirton (doctorate, 1940), who was hired by UC in the Department of Paleontology. Other students receiving advanced degrees also achieved prominence in paleontology. Unfortunately, Matthew died in 1930 with the potential for UCMP unrealized. (Courtesy of UCMP Archives.)

After William Matthew died, Annie Alexander met with the UC president G. Sproul and decided that Charles Camp should be the director of UCMP. Sproul appointed Ralph Chaney as chairman of the Department of Paleontology. Again, Alexander objected to this appointment, believing that Merriam and Chaney wanted control of the museum. She did not like that, fearing her money for the museum would be used by the department from which she wanted complete separation of UCMP. She indicated she would withdraw her funding altogether. Sproul agreed to her demands, and paleontology and the museum were separated with Camp in charge of UCMP. Although Camp served as director from 1930 until 1949, he continued his fieldwork. Camp (left) is shown with his student Reid McDonald and a fossil trackway in New Mexico in 1938. (Courtesy of UCMP Archives.)

In 1930, Annie Alexander approached Sproul again asking for newer and safer facilities for UCMP. The following year he provided space in the Hearst Memorial Mining Building (above) where UCMP would stay for the next 30 years. Fossils were stored and exhibited on the rotunda, shown below with Sam Welles (center) discussing fossils with visitors. During most of this time, UCMP and the Department of Paleontology ran smoothly, with the museum carrying out research and the department tending to academic and administrative functions. Expeditions continued, and the collections grew significantly in invertebrate, vertebrate, and plant paleontology. Micropaleontology too expanded with the radiolarians of Bruce Clark and A.S. Campbell, but foraminifera, a key in the oil industry, remained absent for the most part, in spite of early reports on them in California by W.P. Blake in 1855. (Both, courtesy of UCMP Archives.)

In 1930, Charles Camp and Sam Welles found fossils near St. Johns in eastern Arizona in the Lower Chinle Group of Late Triassic rocks (221–205 mya). This site is called the *Placerias* quarry, after a large herbivorous reptile found there; related to early mammals, it had a stout body, limbs, and powerful neck with a beak to cut vegetation and two short tusks for display or defense. They weighed up to 2,000 kilograms (4,410 pounds) and were 3.5 meters (11.5 feet) long. Forty were found, suggesting that they lived in herds in a calm water body like a lake or slow river. UCMP has revisited the quarry repeatedly, as shown below with faculty curator Kevin Padian and student Laurie Bryant leading a group in 1989 to study and prospect for more fossils. (Both, courtesy of UCMP Archives.)

The Great Depression of 1929–1939 made UCMP activities slower and more difficult, but it also provided additional help through the Works Progress Administration (WPA). Created by Pres. Franklin D. Roosevelt in 1935 when unemployment rose to 20 percent, it was an employment and infrastructure program that employed about 8.5 million Americans until 1943. UCMP benefitted from the WPA by hiring people who sorted and prepared fossils previously collected. At right, Raphael Phoenix prepares a fossil skull in the Hearst Memorial Mining Building around 1940, while another WPA worker below puts the final touches on the preparation of a mammal-like reptile skull from the Karoo Beds of South Africa. (Both, courtesy of UCMP Archives.)

The Black Hawk Quarry, near the southwestern foot of Mount Diablo, was excavated in 1937 by King Arthur Richey (back right) and volunteers, shown here. Students, supervised by Ruben Stirton and Donald Savage, collected fossils or studied there over the next 80 years. The fossils are Late Miocene, 9–10 mya. The area then was a lowland not far from the ocean. The quarry and its fossils are the first appearance of a terrestrial environment after a long history of marine submergence in the area. The fossils include plants (sycamore, elm, poplar, and willow) and vertebrates such as *Gomphotherium* (a relative of the elephant), beavers, horses, camels, rhinoceros, a saber-toothed cat, foxes, dogs, and a crane, which indicated that water was present. All of these are found in beds interleaved in a sequence of sediments deposited in savannah and woodland habitats, perhaps in a riverbed. The quarry site is part of the Trail Through Time at Mount Diablo State Park. UCMP has a large collection of fossils from this site. (Courtesy of UCMP Archives.)

Sam Wells and Ed Cott excavated a fossil dinosaur, later named *Dilophosaurus* by Welles, from a site in Arizona. After discovery of parts of the fossil cropping out of the ground, the remainder of it was uncovered; a jacket was made with wet plaster, burlap, and supporting boards to keep it safe during moving; after it dried, it was removed through considerable effort for transportation to UCMP. Below, Welles shows a reconstruction of the skeleton mounted on a wall in the Earth Science Building in the 1960s. *Dilophosaurus* was the spitting dinosaur that starred in the movie *Jurassic Park*. Welles, after seeing the movie, said, "I thought it might have done that" with glee in his voice. The actual specimen was more than twice as large as the movie version. (Both, courtesy of UCMP Archives.)

UCMP participated in San Francisco's Golden Gate International Exposition in 1939–1940 (left), displaying paleontology to international and American visitors. Starting February 11, 1936, Treasure Island was constructed from dredged sediments in San Francisco Bay. Many exhibits and entertainment venues were built, and artists contributed statues and paintings. UCMP's Charles Camp and William Huff petitioned to include a paleontology exhibit that Huff designed for the science pavilion (below). Huff also designed models for the 20-foot statues representing Industry, Agriculture, Science, and the Arts in niches in the Tower of the Sun; they appear on the stamp honoring the exposition. Guests numbered over 17 million, including 2.5 million from outside California who spent $329 million. It was a huge success for San Francisco and UCMP. (Left, courtesy of the US Postal Service; below, courtesy of UCMP Archives.)

From left to right, Ruben A. Stirton, Carlton Condit, and Samuel P. Welles are dressed in regalia for graduation for their doctorate degrees in 1940. Stirton and Welles, vertebrate paleontologists, went on to join the Department of Paleontology as professor and instructor, while Condit, a paleobotanist, published on Cenozoic plants and fossils of Illinois. Welles later decided not to teach because he would rather collect, prepare, and publish on fossils. (Courtesy of UCMP Archives.)

American involvement in World War II seemed inevitable in 1940; faculty and students became involved after the attack on Pearl Harbor on December 7, 1941. The war shut down paleontology at UCMP entirely. Charles Camp worked with the US Coast Guard; J. Reid Macdonald, a battalion commander on Luzon, returned for a doctorate degree in 1949; Vertress VanderHoof (above center with H. Goeriz, left, in 1942 demonstrating plastering fossils) worked on the Manhattan Project; William Huff (above right) worked at the Alameda Naval Air Station; Donald Savage served six years in the US Air Force in photoreconnaissance and mapping; paleobotanist Daniel Axelrod interpreted aerial photographs for Douglas MacArthur's invasions in the western Pacific islands; and Samuel Welles (below) entered the Engineering Science War Training Program. Coastal California was designated a combat zone, causing concern for the UCMP's fossil collection and remaining paleontologists. (Both, courtesy of UCMP Archives.)

Four

Growing Paleontology

After World War II, faculty and students returned to teach and study paleontology, and UCMP recovered its vitality. The faculty included many of those who had taught prior to the war, but new appointments were made as well. During the war, the safety of the collections was of some concern. Vertress VanderHoof reported: "Attention has already been given to the preservation of type specimens from destruction. Some thought has even been given to the preservation of paleontologists, but they, of course, can be replaced." UCMP and the Department of Paleontology developed a highly regarded research and teaching program. The number of graduate students increased after the war, likely due to support from the GI Bill. Most of them went on to positions in universities and museums across America. All fields of paleontology—micropaleontology, paleobotany, invertebrate paleontology, and vertebrate paleontology—were built into a strong center in all divisions of the subject. The new faculty, R.M. Kleinpell, D. Savage, and J.W. Durham, joined Camp and Chaney in the department, and with Ruben Stirton and Sam Welles in the museum, formed a large and powerful group with high reputations in paleontology. Annie Alexander and her partner Louise Kellogg added plants to their collecting plans. They collected for many months in the West and Mexico, donating the plants to the University Herbarium. This and other diversions caused Alexander to become less involved in the ordinary operations of the museum. She still maintained an interest in and support for UCMP, although paleontology was now mostly on its own. In 1950, Annie Alexander passed away at age 82.

By 1955, the Department of Paleontology and UCMP was complete again with eight paleontologists. They covered all aspects of paleontology—paleobotany, invertebrate, vertebrate, and micropaleontology. From left to right are (first row) Donald E. Savage, vertebrate paleontology; Ralph L. Langenheim, invertebrate paleontology; Sam Welles, vertebrate paleontology; and J. Wyatt Durham, invertebrate paleontology; (second row) Ralph W. Chaney, paleobotany; Ruben A. Stirton, mammalian paleontology; Robert M. Kleinpell, micropaleontology; and Charles L. Camp, reptilian paleontology. Welles was an instructor in the department but resigned to be a full-time museum paleontologist so he could collect, prepare, and publish on fossils. Langenheim was assistant professor from 1952 until 1959 and then joined the geology department at the University of Illinois, Urbana. The rest spent their entire lives at Berkeley. The Department of Paleontology was the only such department in America; paleontology elsewhere was taught in the geology or biology departments and none of them covered so much of the field. With both a department and a museum, Berkeley was regarded as the premier place to learn about the discipline at the graduate level. (Courtesy of UCMP Archives.)

Artist William Gordon Huff (1903–1993), shown at right in 1980, was born in Fresno, California, developed a childhood interest in art, and moved with his family to Oakland in 1918. After graduating high school in 1923, his first commission came for two 15-foot statues of Greek goddesses for a play at UC's Greek Theatre. He then went to New York, Paris, and Italy; married; then drove to Berkeley where he met Charles Camp and became a close friend of UCMP. He did sculptures, drawings, and paintings of many subjects but especially of fossils and their reconstructions individually and in their ancient environments. He made casts of *Placerias* for Camp, reconstructed the head of the giant Pleistocene *Bison latifrons* (below) for the UCMP exhibit at the Golden Gate International Exposition, and created a bas-relief ichthyosaur wall at Berlin-Ichthyosaur State Park in Nevada. (Both, courtesy of UCMP Archives.)

Charles Camp (1893–1972) was born in Jamestown, North Dakota, and two years later, his family moved to Sierra Madre, California. He collected fossils in Bridger Basin, Wyoming, and worked on Rancho La Brea fossils as an undergraduate at Berkeley. After receiving a doctorate degree from Columbia University in 1923, he took positions in zoology and later at UCMP in Berkeley. He was an inveterate fossil collector and found vertebrates across the West and in South Africa and Australia. Returning from his World War II duties, he restarted his collecting and publishing activities as well as training a continuing line of vertebrate paleontologists. His interests were wide and included history of the West and of paleontology as well as book collecting. He was one of the foremost American reptilian paleontologists at the time. Camp, seen here examining a fossil in Monument Valley, continued his research on fossil reptiles at other sites in Arizona. He wrote outstanding descriptive and interpretive monographs and papers on various fossil reptiles. As a longtime director of UCMP, he brought order to the paleontology program. (Courtesy of UCMP Archives.)

Ralph Chaney remained a faculty member in the department and a faculty curator in UCMP. He worked on the fossil floras of the West and taught paleobotany from 1931 to 1957. The history of redwoods in North America was a major interest of his. In addition to the coast redwood and sequoia, a third species of redwood, the poorly understood dawn redwood (*Metasequoia glyptostroboides*), was abundant in the fossil record. During the Tertiary, the tree was widespread throughout North America, Asia, and Greenland. Scientists thought it had been extinct for at least 20 million years based on its fossils, and no one had seen it alive. In 1944, dawn redwoods were found growing in the Sichuan province of China. In 1948, a group from the Save the Redwoods League, including future league president Ralph Chaney, visited China (leaning against a huge dawn redwood at right) and found thousands of them growing in lowland canyons. The dawn redwood is now grown chiefly from seeds worldwide as a beautiful garden plant. (Courtesy of UCMP Archives.)

Ruben Stirton (1901–1966) worked for William Matthew at UCMP since 1930, received his doctorate degree in 1940 on the evolution of horses, and was later appointed professor (1949), chair of the Department of Paleontology (1951–1956), and director of UCMP (1949–1966). He continued an outstanding program of mammalian paleontology, teaching, and campus activities. Above, he checks a drawing against the specimen. His interests in fossil mammals included beavers, horses, and marsupials and their evolution, biogeography, and value in stratigraphy. Fascinated with marsupials, he organized expeditions (1953–1966) to collect in Australia. Little was known of Australian fossil mammals; Stirton and his teams found and published on nine new occurrences and dozens of new species of mammals. His fieldwork broadened the UCMP mammal collections. Below, he consults with the "Boy Paleontologists" about their finds in Fremont, California. (Above, courtesy of UCMP Archives; below, courtesy of Math Science Nucleus.)

Robert M. Kleinpell (1905–1986) published his classic *The Miocene Stratigraphy of California* in 1938 based on his 1934 doctorate dissertation at Stanford University. He worked on a variety of geological problems for oil companies, particularly in the southwest Pacific island nations. In Manila, he was captured in 1942 by enemy forces and interred for three years. During that time, he taught children in the camps biology and geology. Returning to California, he was appointed to the UC faculty and UCMP in 1946. His work on foraminiferal biostratigraphy was a fundamental exploration tool for the thriving oil industry. Until his retirement in 1974, he produced a long line of students in micropaleontology as well as influential and important publications on fossil foraminifera and biostratigraphy of California. He and his students developed a very large collection of foraminiferal samples and slides, filling cabinets (seen here in 2000) that formed an outstanding resource in foraminiferal work. Kleinpell was regarded as the foremost Californian micropaleontologist by the oil industry and academia and as a historian of the field itself. (Author's collection.)

J. Wyatt Durham (1907–1996), an invertebrate paleontologist, received his doctorate degree in 1941 under Bruce Clark at UCMP on Oligocene megafossils from Washington. He worked as a petroleum geologist in Java and Sumatra from 1936 to 1939 and Colombia from 1943 to 1946. Durham then joined the UC faculty and UCMP in 1947; he and his students studied invertebrates, their biostratigraphy, paleoecology, and evolution. He had strong doubts about continental drift and plate tectonics. (Courtesy of Carole Hickman.)

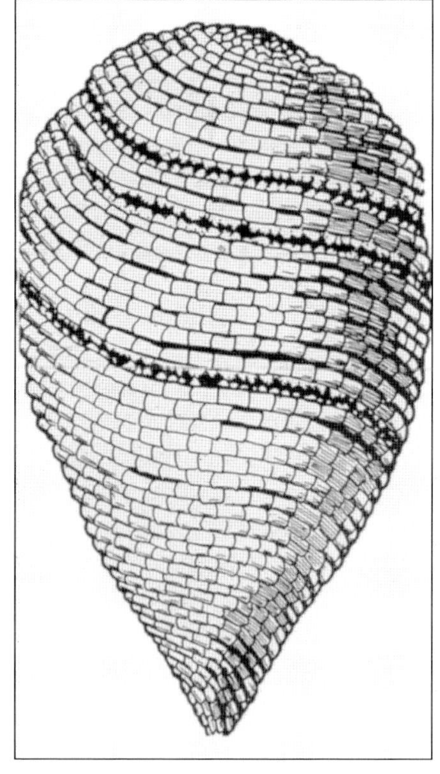

One of Durham's most significant contributions was his study of strange fossils from the White Mountains of eastern California first found by two students in 1962. Durham and student Roland Gangloff collected 20 specimens from lower Cambrian rocks; Durham and colleagues described it as *Helicoplacus* (pictured here, 2.5 cm, 1 inch long) in a new class of echinoderms. Durham was president of the Paleontological Society and received the Paleontological Society Medal in 1988. (Courtesy of UCMP Archives.)

Donald Savage (1917–1999), shown here preparing a fossil, continued on as a faculty member after finishing his doctorate in 1949 under Ruben Stirton in the Department of Paleontology. His interests initially focused on the description and stratigraphy of mammalian faunas throughout the West, which he began as a student at the University of Oklahoma. Savage was particularly concerned with the radiometric ages of the vertebrate faunas of western North America and worked with geologists to obtain those dates from volcanic rocks associated with the fossils. His work expanded internationally to South America, France, and Burma. He was also an expert on making displays of fossils. Once, he made a cast from a natural mold of an extinct rhinoceros overcome in an ancient lava flow exposed along the Columbia River. He was director of UCMP from 1966 to 1971 and president of the Society of Vertebrate Paleontology. He too had a number of outstanding students in paleontology and geology. After retirement, he took a temporary position (1995) making fossil displays at the University of Oklahoma Museum of Natural History. (Courtesy of UCMP Archives.)

Sam Welles (1909–1997), who received his doctorate in paleontology in 1940 at Berkeley, specialized in reptiles and worked closely with Charles Camp in the field, although he treasured his own numerous and major contributions. Welles, shown at left cleaning vertebrae at Ichthyosaur State Park, believed that the chief goal of a paleontologist was to collect fossils in the field before natural processes destroyed them, and he was very good at that, having collected and prepared many of the larger vertebrate fossils at UCMP. (Courtesy of UCMP Archives.)

Welles described the plesiosaur *Hydrotherosaurus alexandrae* he found near Panoche Pass, California, in 1937 and named it after Annie Alexander, much to her annoyance as she did not want honors for her support. Among many other accomplishments, he found and described the dinosaur *Dilophosaurus* in Arizona. (Courtesy of UCMP Archives.)

Wes Gordon of Hayward, California, organized and led a group of 16 young boys in the 1940s to collect fossils in Fremont (right). The group became world famous when *Life* magazine's December 1945 issue featured them and called them the "Boy Paleontologists of Fremont." The name stuck. Ruben Stirton, Donald Savage, and J.W. Durham of UCMP were invited by Gordon to help with handling and identifying the fossils. The paleontologists were interested and supportive because the fossils the boys discovered represented a time in the Pleistocene ice ages previously undescribed; Savage thus named this time from 1.6 to 0.25 mya the Irvingtonian after the Irvington District in Fremont. The vertebrate fossils included mammoths (a tusk of one is shown below), horses, and other large herbivores. The boys recovered 20,000 fossils, which are now mostly at UCMP. (Both, courtesy of Math Science Nucleus.)

Annie Alexander fell ill in October 1949. Louise Kellogg took her to a hospital in Oakland. She demanded to go home where Kellogg could cook for her. In November, Alexander returned to the hospital, followed by a major stroke. She was comatose for the next 10 months and died on September 10, 1950, at age 82. Her ashes were buried by Louise Kellogg in Makawao Cemetery, Maui, near her childhood home in Ha'iku. Alexander and Kellogg had shared their lives, values, fascination with nature and the outdoors, and love for 42 years. Both are celebrated on the Berkeley campus as "Gay Bears," although neither would welcome that, as they always eschewed any recognition for their work or lives. Alexander founded the Museum of Vertebrate Zoology in 1908 and the Museum of Paleontology in 1921. She and Kellogg also contributed many specimens to the museums and thousands of plants to the University Herbarium. Alexander endowed UCMP first in March 1934, then in August 1934, December 1945, and July 1948. (Courtesy of UCMP Archives.)

Berlin-Ichthyosaur, a 1,153-acre Nevada state park in the Shoshone Mountains, was established to protect the ghost town of Berlin and the ichthyosaur fossil deposits nearby (above). The ichthyosaurs, marine lizards known throughout the Mesozoic, are found in a bone bed deposited about 225 mya during the Triassic period. From 1953 to 1958, Charles Camp, assisted by Sam Welles in 1953, devoted summers to excavating the giants from the bed. Camp found over 40 animals and documented the uniqueness of the occurrence. He lived in the cabin (below) built with wood from the nearby ghost town of Berlin. Camp persuaded the State of Nevada to make the site a state park where the skeletons were left in the rocks as a field museum under a sturdy shelter. (Both, author's collection.)

At Berlin-Ichthyosaur State Park, the exhibition building protects bones and skeletons still embedded in the rock (above). Other specimens were removed by the paleontologists for research and are at the UCMP where students and faculty curators have studied them. With Camp's encouragement and guidance, artist William Huff designed and helped construct the bas-relief ichthyosaur wall (below) that greets visitors to the park. The ichthyosaur *Shonisaurus popular*i, the largest ichthyosaur known at the time, was designated the Nevada state fossil in 1977. (Both, author's collection.)

The Earth Sciences Building (above), later renamed McCone Hall, was opened in 1960 to house the geology and paleontology departments and UCMP. The paleontology faculty and students occupied the first and second floors with fossil displays on the walls (shown below during an open house), while UCMP was in the basement with storage and preparation labs. Geology took the upper floors. A seismograph was on the ground floor and was a focus of interest just after the Loma Prieta earthquake. In 1989, the Department of Paleontology was merged with the new Department of Integrative Biology but remained in McCone Hall. In 1995, the old paleontology department and the Museum of Paleontology moved into the newly reconstructed Valley Life Sciences Building (VLSB). (Above, author's collection; below, courtesy of UCMP Archives.)

Joseph T. Gregory (1914–2007) was named a professor in the Department of Paleontology and UCMP in 1960 after a long career in vertebrate paleontology at the American Museum of Natural History, the University of Michigan, and the Peabody Museum at Yale. Berkeley was a return to his roots—he did a doctorate dissertation on Pliocene vertebrates from South Dakota in 1938 under Ruben Stirton. Gregory was chair of the department (1960–1965) and director of the museum (1971–1975). His interests were chiefly in Triassic reptiles and the history of paleontology. Gregory took field trips with students to the Black Hawk Quarry, Shark Tooth Hill, Pyramid Hill (above in 1964) near Bakersfield, and Montana, where they collected the large *Tricerotops* skull displayed in the library. He knew the Black Hawk Quarry was a treasure to be saved. With the Black Hawk Ranch up for sale, Gregory negotiated with the buyers to give the quarry to the university, which they did. He drew plans for an outdoor exhibit, and although that was never realized, the quarry became part of the Trail Through Time. (Author's collection.)

A bone bed at Shark Tooth Hill (seen here in 1960) near Bakersfield, California, yields abundant marine vertebrate fossils. W.P. Blake, of the California Academy of Sciences, found fossil shark teeth near here in 1852 and sent them to Louis Agassiz at Harvard. He described eight new sharks in 1856, the first paper on vertebrate fossils from the Pacific coast. (Author's collection.)

The Shark Tooth Hill bone bed is fairly hard and requires considerable effort, exerted by a volunteer here in 1960, to extract the fossil shark teeth, seals, sea lions, whales and porpoises, a sea cow (*Desmostylus*), and a few terrestrial mammals. Recent UCMP research indicates the bone bed formed over a long time, allowing the skeletons and teeth to accumulate. It has been an important site for UCMP paleontologists since 1912. (Author's collection.)

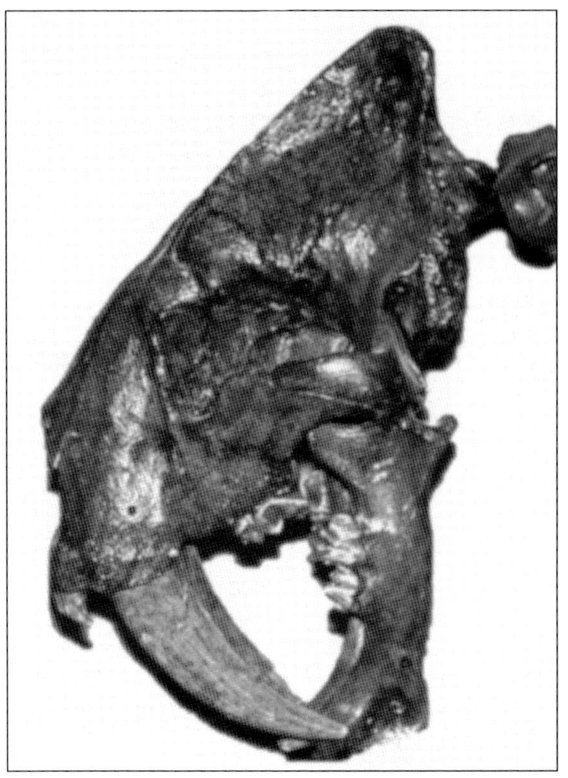

The saber-toothed cat (*Smilodon californicus*) was officially adopted as the California state fossil in 1973, thanks to faculty curator Donald Savage's efforts. Its fossils are common in late Pleistocene deposits of the state. The skull from Rancho La Brea is 12.6 inches long; upper canine teeth can be up to eight inches long. It became extinct 10,000 to 11,000 years ago. (Courtesy of UCMP.)

A reconstruction of a saber-toothed cat sits outside the south entrance to the Earth Sciences Building, now called McCone Hall. The statue was sculpted in 1975 by Victor Bergeron—"Trader Vic"—to celebrate the state fossil. California also had a state dinosaur designated in 2017—*Augustynolophus morrisi*, a hadrosaur or "duck-billed dinosaur." It occurs in California deposits 66 mya (late Cretaceous). (Author's collection.)

Professor and faculty curator Bill Clemens (1932–2020), along with faculty, staff, graduate and undergraduate students, and research associates, led decades of fieldwork in Cretaceous rocks in eastern Montana beginning in the early 1970s and continuing today. Sitting on Clemens's Chevy Blazer at Jordan, Montana, in 1979 are, from left to right, (first row) Mark Goodwin (UCMP), Cathy Engdahl, Mike Greenwald (UCMP), and Lowell Dingus (UCMP); (second row) Jane, Bob, and Duane Engdahl; Clemens (UCMP); and Dave Archibald (UCMP alum). The Engdahl family are longtime supporters of UCMP and fieldwork on their ranch in Jordan. Clemens inspired students in the field and lab; today, they hold positions in various universities and museums. Among those are Dave Polly (left below) and Mark Goodwin seen excavating fossils from a Cretaceous exposure in Clemens territory in Montana in 1990. (Both, courtesy of Mark Goodwin.)

Prof. Zach Arnold (left), a faculty curator who worked in protozoology, talks with German biologist Rudolf Röttger at the Forams 1994 meeting hosted by UCMP. Along with Robert Kleinpell, Arnold, who received his UCMP doctorate in 1948, researched the biology of single-celled foraminifera, focusing on the reproductive cycles of several species. Arnold and Kleinpell realized an understanding of the living organisms would enable better interpretations of fossil foraminifera. Arnold joined UCMP in 1957 and retired in 1978. (Courtesy of UCMP Archives.)

Five

Paleobiology and Outreach

In the late 1970s, paleobiology began to focus on the biology of fossils rather than their description and stratigraphy, which had dominated earlier studies. Of course, some paleontologists, including those at UCMP, always interpreted the biology of their fossils and habitats, and many paleontologists continued to describe specimens and their occurrences in time and space, yet paleobiology proved a boost for paleontology. At Berkeley, paleontologists moved in that direction, and the appointment of new faculty to UCMP broke new ground working on topics like the feeding strategies of ancient animals, the distribution of plants through time, the biology of the first animals, distribution in time in relation to climate change, examination of functional morphology, the origin of flight, and of the carrying capacity of the land for *Tyrannosaurus rex*, among others. New techniques and instrumentation were also brought to bear on these new problems—isotopic analyses, scanning electron microscopy, geochemistry, and molecular biology undertaken at UCMP. The research required study in UCMP collections and more fieldwork. UCMP paleontologists and students collaborated with scientists in foreign countries. Graduate student enrollments went up, including an increase in women. Over 425 students, including 110 women, earned master of art or doctorate degrees from 1904 to 2020 and took positions in various universities, colleges, museums, and industries.

UCMP had always done outreach activities, like the annual open house, the Boy Paleontologists, and public participation in expeditions, but a renewed effort began in 1994 with an assistant director devoted to outreach and education. This brought K–12 teachers, college students, and even scientists to take special workshops on teaching techniques. For professionals, UCMP hosted meetings on mollusks, foraminifera, and paleobiology with attendances up to 650. In 1993, UCMP graduate students developed one of the first 30–50 websites. The Behring Institute and museum invited UC Berkeley to establish exhibits. By 1991, UCMP had installed displays of its fossils along with special activities for its audiences, like the family dig at Black Hawk Quarry. UCMP also initiated a Trek Through Time that started in the Jurassic and ended in the Miocene at the base of Mt. Diablo.

Prof. Carole Hickman, who received her doctorate from Stanford in 1974, was the first woman faculty curator at UCMP in 1976, where she researches and teaches invertebrate paleontology and functional morphology. Here, she compares a modern *Turbo* snail (left) to a fossil. She regularly worked on Oregon and Washington fossils but led two expeditions to the Galapagos Islands (1982 and 1986). Fossils collected from 187 localities indicated the islands appeared no more than 4 mya. (Courtesy of UCMP Archives.)

In 1982, Carole Hickman and her student Matt James explore a reef suddenly raised from the sea in 1954 by movements of magma within an active volcano at Urvina Bay, Isla Isabela, Galapagos Islands. The deposit contains corals, mollusks, echinoderms, and other animals. Such occurrences indicate caution is necessary when documenting the ages of fossil deposits. (Author's collection.)

In 1991, Jim Valentine and the author established a long-term collaboration with PIN, Russia's Paleontological Institute (above), in Moscow. The collaboration developed into the acquisition of fossils of the first animals; exchange of directors, scientists, and students; web assistance for PIN; field trips to the White Sea, Siberia, and Kazakhstan; and collaborative research and lectures at PIN and UCMP. Valentine (below, left) is pictured at dinner with Russian colleagues in a private home in Moscow before going to the White Sea, a branch of the Arctic Ocean in the far north of Russia, to prospect for late Precambrian fossils 550–600 mya. On later trips, students and volunteers camped at Bear Creek adjacent to the White Sea. (Both, author's collection.)

At Russia's Paleontological Institute (PIN) in September 1993, UCMP students assisting PIN's network administrator with web development are Dave Polly (left), Ben Waggoner (second from left), and Rob Guralnick (right). UCMP hosted the PIN website on its servers. Waggoner spent a year in Moscow studying fossils of the first animals dating around 550 mya; he finished his 1997 doctorate at UCMP. Below, Polly and Waggoner explore Red Square in central Moscow. (Both, courtesy of Dave Polly.)

Students and members of the University Research Expeditions prospected the cliffs along the White Sea (above) in search of fossils of the earliest animals. PIN paleontologist M.A. Fedonkin led the expeditions for several years and assisted in further visits to PIN to study the collected fossils and those in Fedonkin's extensive collection. These enigmatic fossils occur worldwide but are much different than younger fossils or modern animals. Some of them were interpreted as jellyfish but later determined to be the holdfasts of frond-like organisms (right, 8.5 cm long) extending into the water above the seafloor. Others apparently laid or were squashed on the bottom, which was covered in a firm algal mat. Fossils from this coast are more than 550 million years old. (Both, author's collection.)

In 1988, the Blackhawk Museum (above), a collaboration with UC Berkeley, was established by Kenneth Behring, developer of the Blackhawk community near Danville, California. UC Berkeley cooperated in planning two galleries, one on paleontology and another on anthropology, adjacent to the main attraction, a superb collection of automobiles. A plan was begun by director W. Berry in 1985 and brought to fruition between 1989 and 1991 by D. Savage, M. Goodwin, and author Jere Lipps working with exhibit designers and UCMP faculty curators and staff. The exhibit, In Pursuit of Ancient Life, featured fossils from the region, including a gomphothere (an early elephant). Savage (below, left) assembles a desmostylian (like a sea cow) for the exhibit. The gallery opened in 1991 and closed six years later; annual attendance was over 50,000, including schoolchildren. (Above, author's collection; below, courtesy of UCMP Archives.)

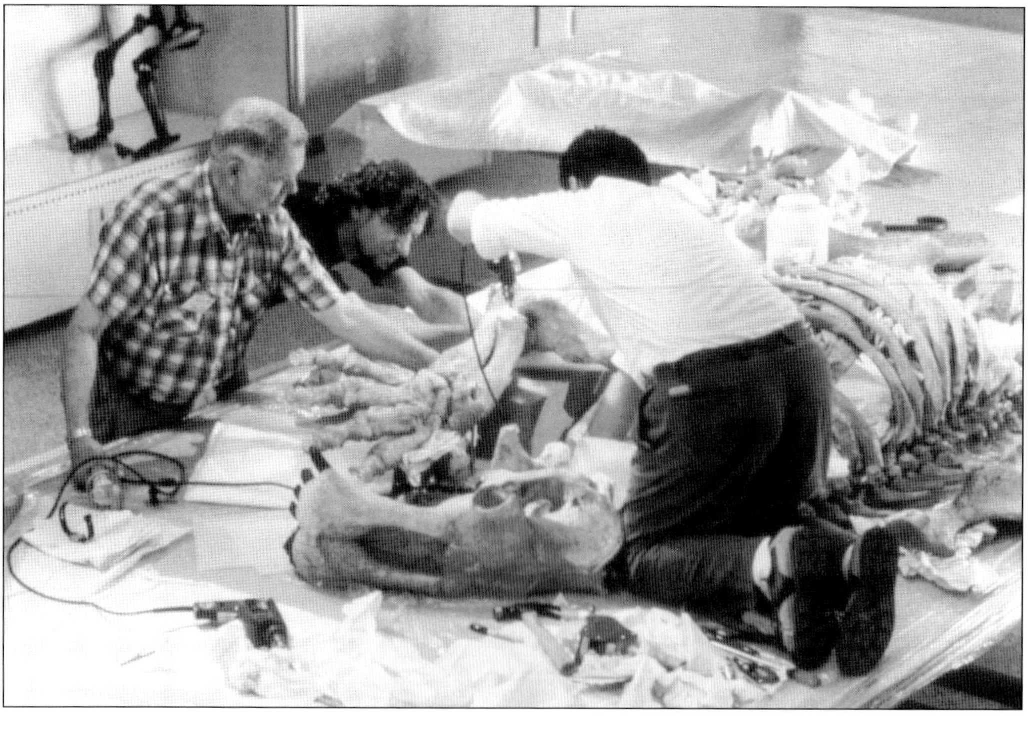

UCMP's home now is the VLSB, which houses four museums, the Bioscience Library, classrooms, laboratories, and offices. When it was first constructed in 1930, it was the largest university building in the nation and housed all the life sciences at Berkeley except paleontology. In the late 1980s, a university-wide reorganization of the life sciences included the reconstruction of the interior of the VLSB. Bulldozers and dump trucks moved in and out of a hole in the side of the building where none had been before. At the same time (1989), biology at Berkeley was reorganized into fewer departments, including the merging of paleontology into the new Department of Integrative Biology. It and UCMP moved into the building in 1995. The museum occupies a large space on the lower floor. (Author's collection.)

The *Tyrannosaurus rex* in the atrium of VLSB is UCMP's icon (above with Mark Goodwin, right, and Jere Lipps). When Dean David Bentley visited the empty VLSB, he asked Lipps, who was UCMP director, "What will go in this space?" "How about a *T. rex*?" said the director, having no idea where to get one. The dean said, "Fantastic." The director asked Mark Goodwin, "Can we get a *T. rex*?" Goodwin replied, "Sure!" Soon they were at the Museum of the Rockies in Bozeman, Montana. They got epoxy resin cast reproductions of bones found by Montana rancher and amateur fossil collector Kathy Wankel in 1988 weathering from the Late Cretaceous Hell Creek Formation on Federal Bureau of Reclamation land. Perched on a lift, Mark Siegel (below, left) and Mark Goodwin (below, right) attach the skull to the skeleton. Berkeley undergraduate Athena Trakadas steadies the skull with a guideline. Assembly took the summer of 1995. The original skeleton, now known as "The Nation's *T. rex*," is displayed at the National Museum of Natural History in Washington, DC. (Above, author's collection; below, courtesy of Mark Goodwin.)

Chancellor Chang-Lien Tien was invited to open the *T. rex* display in the fall of 1995. He showed up with his usual enthusiasm, toured the collections asking, "Are we number one in paleontology yet?" The answer had to be yes, of course, or he would have been very disappointed. He and Jere Lipps, then director, cut the ribbon on the stairs leading to the *T. rex*. Everyone was excited to see it and wanted to be involved. So, an opportunity to "Own a Piece of the Rex" was developed, with each bone having a price from a few dollars for a toe bone to over $500 for the skull. A chart indicated who "owned" which piece. The funds were used to develop the exhibit. The dinosaur became a regular stop on university tours, especially those for incoming students and special visitors. Apart from being the center of CalDay events, it is also discussed in lecture classes, sometimes with an assignment, and it can be used by researchers to explore dinosaur anatomy and function. (Courtesy of UCMP.)

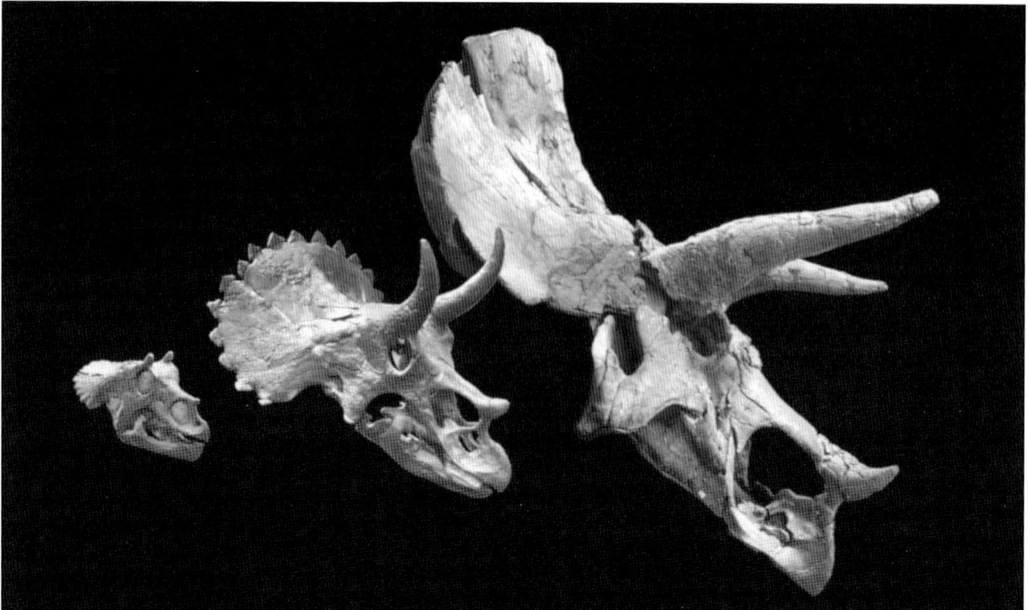

Three skulls of *Triceratops* on display in the Marian Koshland Bioscience, Natural Resources, & Public Health Library illustrate the extreme changes that occur during growth or ontogeny. The specimens were collected in Montana by UCMP crews over a decade. Mark Goodwin and Jack Horner demonstrated that the horns are short and straight in babies (left), curve backwards in juveniles (center), and then recurve forward in adults (right). (Courtesy of Paul Hudson.)

The largest specimen of *Triceratops* was prepared by gluing fragments together, a job taking Coco Kishi over a year to finish. Below, she sits (right) with Goodwin (left) and Clemens on an outcrop in Stewarts Valley, Nevada, collecting fossil insects. (Courtesy of UCMP Archives.)

Judy Scotchmoor volunteered at UCMP in the fossil prep lab in 1993 and became director of education and public programs in 1994. Taking advantage of her K–12 teaching experiences, she initiated teacher professional development workshops, field trips, and curricula focused on evolution and the process of science. Scotchmoor led development of two award-winning websites, Understanding Evolution and Understanding Science, on the UCMP website that have been seen by thousands of visitors. She assisted in the planning of the Trail Through Time at Mount Diablo and organized several Treks Through Time that drew hundreds of participants. As an organizer of UCMP's open house during the annual CalDay, Scotchmoor welcomed people to learn about paleontology and UCMP. Pictured here along the Colville River in Alaska on a research expedition, she works with Oakland, California, schoolteachers prospecting and excavating dinosaurs. (Courtesy of Roland Gangloff.)

UCMP paleontologists have always recognized the importance of many of the places they worked. They became involved in establishing some of these places as national parks or monuments and state and local parks, starting with LeConte working with Muir in the late 1800s to get Yosemite National Park recognized. Others have also made similar efforts: Merriam with John Day National Monument, Camp with Berlin-Ichthyosaur State Park, and Harry MacGinitie with Florissant Fossil Beds National Monument, to name a few. Annie Alexander saw Muir's fossils from the Petrified Forest National Monument (now a park) and made her own collecting trip there in 1921. Camp then followed with several trips by car (pictured) in the 1920s to collect more reptile fossils for his study of phytosaurs in the monument and elsewhere in Arizona. UCMP cares for 14,695 fossil specimens from 952 localities in 47 national parks and many more from state parks in several states. It has provided casts of fossils for exhibits in various parks and other universities. (Courtesy of UCMP Archives.)

Anthony Barnosky, faculty curator at UCMP from 1990 to 2016, works on fossil mammals. For him, the fossil record illustrates and communicates how much humans have changed the planet. His teaching emphasized experiential learning in field paleontology to global change dynamics. His group contributed thousands of specimens to UCMP, primarily from Miocene outcrops in Montana and Idaho and Pleistocene Porcupine Cave in Colorado. Barnosky advised state, national, and international policy makers on scientific issues, wrote books for the public, and appeared in films that highlighted solutions to world issues like climate change and the extinction crisis (*Tomorrow*, 2016 César Award for Best Documentary Film, and *Animal*, 2021 Cannes Film Festival). At right, Barnosky excavates fossils at Samwell Cave above Lake Shasta, California, in 2008; below is dinner with students while camping in Nevada in 2003. (Both, courtesy of Jessica Blois and Faysal Bibi.)

Prof. Leslea Hlusko, shown here at Olduvai Gorge, Tanzania, in June 2012, directed field projects in eastern Africa: in Kenya (2000–2007) at the Late Miocene site of Lemudong'o (7 mya) and in Tanzania with the Tanzanian International Paleoanthropological Research Project (2006–present) and the Olduvai Vertebrate Paleontology Project (2011–2015). She also participated in fieldwork in Ethiopia, Turkey, and Wyoming. She has served as the advisor for six UC Berkeley doctorate projects in integrative biology, all awarded to women and/or other historically underrepresented groups in the sciences. She is also currently a research professor at the National Research Center on Human Evolution in Spain. (Both photographs by Whitney Reiner.)

Professor Hlusko works with students from UC Berkeley and universities in Africa. Here, with her back to the camera, she discusses field strategies with her student Theresa Greico (PhD, 2013) and field assistants while goats watch at Olduvai Gorge, Tanzania, in June 2012. Below, Sarah Kigama Amugongo Hanang excavates fossils one million years old at Mount Hanang, Tanzania, in September 2007. Originally from Kenya, a colleague at the University of Nairobi introduced her to Hlusko, and she then helped at the Late Miocene site Lemudong'o. Hanang came to Berkeley for her doctorate in 2010. Her interests are in how prenatal factors influence bone development, and she is on the faculty at the University of Minnesota College of Veterinary Medicine. (Above, courtesy of Whitney Reiner; below, courtesy of L. Hlusko.)

Professor and faculty curator Jack Tseng (above, right) examines a fossil mammal skull (Miocene, about 12 mya) with doctoral student Sergio Garcia-Lara (left) and research associate Avi Berger beside an X-ray nanoCT System in their research laboratory. The system takes 3D pictures of fossil and biological specimens to aid in understanding their relationships, functions, and evolution. Tseng's doctoral students, two postdoctoral scientists, and three undergraduates use the CT system to study subjects ranging from chewing in extinct mammals, brain evolution, and olfactory system form to whole-skeleton form-function relationships. Below, on a field trip to the Mohave Desert, Tseng points out the geology to his students. (Both, courtesy of Jack Tseng.)

The author discusses the genetics and paleontology of cypraeid snails collected across the Pacific with his student Chris Meyer (PhD, 1992), now of the Smithsonian Institution. Meyer pioneered the sequencing of genes in the genetics lab newly established in UCMP. Genes provide another history of organisms that complements those determined by fossils and thus is extremely important. (Courtesy of UCMP Archives.)

The author studies modern marine biology and ecology to help interpret ancient fossil occurrences. Here, in 1994, he was in Jellyfish Lake, Palau, where jellyfish are very abundant, and the water column becomes anoxic and sulfurous below 15 meters (49.5 feet). The sediment above and in the anoxic zone preserves certain structures and organisms similar to those found in Precambrian and Cambrian fossil occurrences elsewhere in the world. (Author's collection.)

In 1980, Prof. Walter Alvarez, Department of Earth and Planetary Sciences and curatorial associate in UCMP, together with his father, Luis Alvarez, Nobel Prize laureate in Physics; Frank Asaro; and Helen Michel proposed that an asteroid hit Earth causing an ecologic catastrophe, killing off the dinosaurs and other animals 66 mya. The evidence came from the abundance of iridium in the sediments, an element that is rare on the surface of Earth but present in asteroids. Here, Alvarez (center) with his students Mark Anders (left) and Dave Bice examine an outcrop at Gubbio, Italy, where fossil, rock, and geochemical evidence indicates the place of the impact at the top of the white bed. The idea started an avalanche of research that continues to this day. Evidence supports not only the hypothesis but revealed where the asteroid hit Earth on the Yucatan Peninsula of Mexico. (Courtesy of Walter Alvarez.)

Doris Sloan, associate curator in UCMP and a faculty member in the Department of Earth and Planetary Sciences, is pictured on the Trail Through Time in 1995. She authored an informative book on the geology of the San Francisco Bay Area. Her chief research interest is fossil foraminifera, especially to reconstruct the ancient environments of San Francisco Bay for the last 200,000 years or so. (Author's collection.)

The Trail Through Time, originated by UCMP in 1995, extends from the top of Mount Diablo to its base and traverses 150 million years of time from the Jurassic to the Miocene. Signs along the way, developed by geologists like Doris Sloan, explain the geology and paleontology at critical intervals. Here, a guide explains the history and development of the mountain. (Author's collection.)

Age dating is critical to paleontology. Paul Renne, director of the Berkeley Geochronology Center and UCMP associate, and his students provide dates and interpret their significance. Renne (right) and doctoral student Courtney Sprain, pictured in the Berkeley Geochronology Center, measure ages from volcanic ash at the Cretaceous-Paleogene boundary, Hell Creek region, Montana. This region is renowned for abundant dinosaur fossils, their extinction 66 mya, and insights into the following radiation of mammals. (Courtesy of Paul Renne.)

The end of the Cretaceous marked the extinction of the dinosaurs and much of the rest of life on Earth by an asteroid impact and volcanism. The boundary between this period and the Paleogene, shown here, is measured at 66 mya. (Courtesy of Paul Renne.)

The director of education and outreach, Lisa White runs UCMP programs for K–12 and college students and the public. Here, she is on the deep-sea drilling vessel *JOIDES Resolution* during the July 2017 School of Rock instructional cruise for educators and early career International Ocean Discovery Program (IODP) scientists. During transit from Subic Bay, Philippines, to the Coral Sea, Australia, White and IODP scientists showcased the ship's capabilities with the goal of increasing the diversity of those who apply to sail on IODP and other expeditions in the future. White works to build a diverse mentoring pool for undergraduate geoscience students and to create and expand partnerships bolstering pathways to STEM careers. White, a micropaleontologist, is shown sampling cores retrieved from the seafloor for diatom microfossils, which help her interpret paleoceanography and paleoclimates of past times. (Courtesy of Lisa White.)

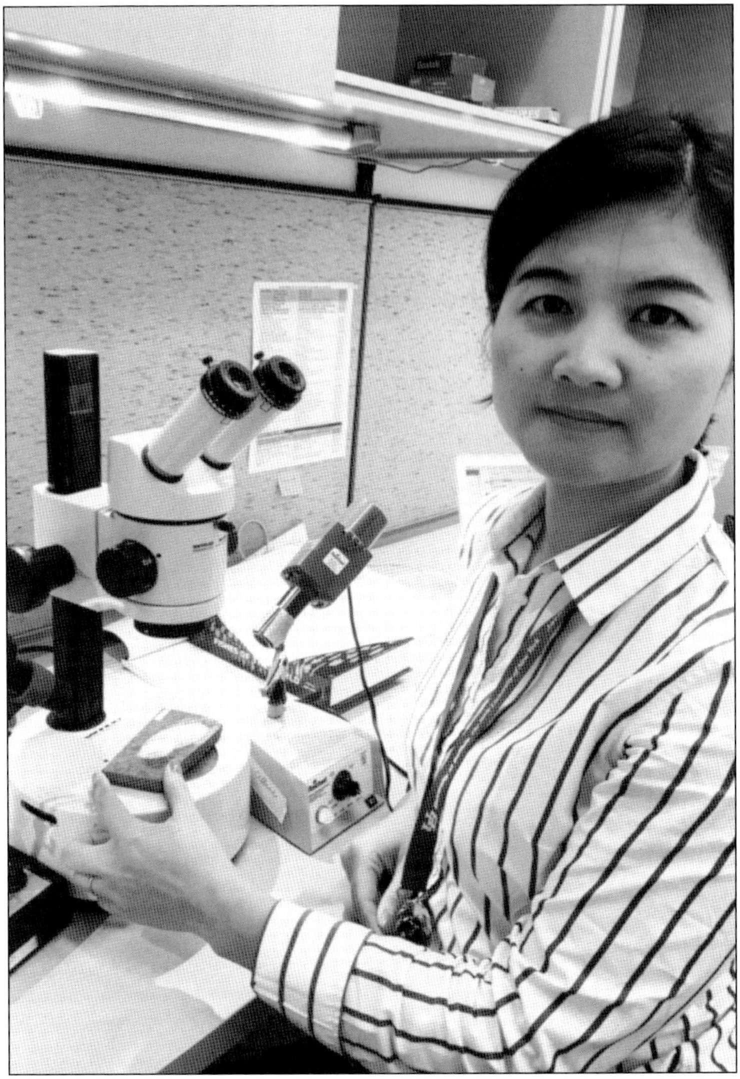

Juan Liu, assistant curator at UCMP (2020–) is interested in fossil fishes, a topic not well studied at UCMP in the past. She earned her master of science degree in the Institute of Vertebrate Paleontology and Paleoanthropology, China, and her doctorate degree at the University of Alberta, Canada. Liu now oversees a research lab focused on systematic paleontology of fossil fishes and functional anatomy of vertebrate auditory systems. Liu prospects field localities with outstanding fish fossils and delights in studying fish in deep time. She sits at the microscope in her lab used to see details of her fossils (left). Below is one of Liu's favorite fish fossils, a carp-like fish nine centimeters long (3.5 inches) from the Eocene of south China. (Both, courtesy of Jack Tseng.)

Paleobotanist Diane M. Erwin, museum scientist, shows plant fossils to visitors inside UCMP on CalDay 2012. Her research focuses on the always changing western North American Tertiary plant communities and their evolution, form, and distributions. Erwin combines research with curation, improving the scientific, teaching, and outreach values of the fossils. She chose her career because the geological history of plants was fascinating. (Courtesy of UCMP.)

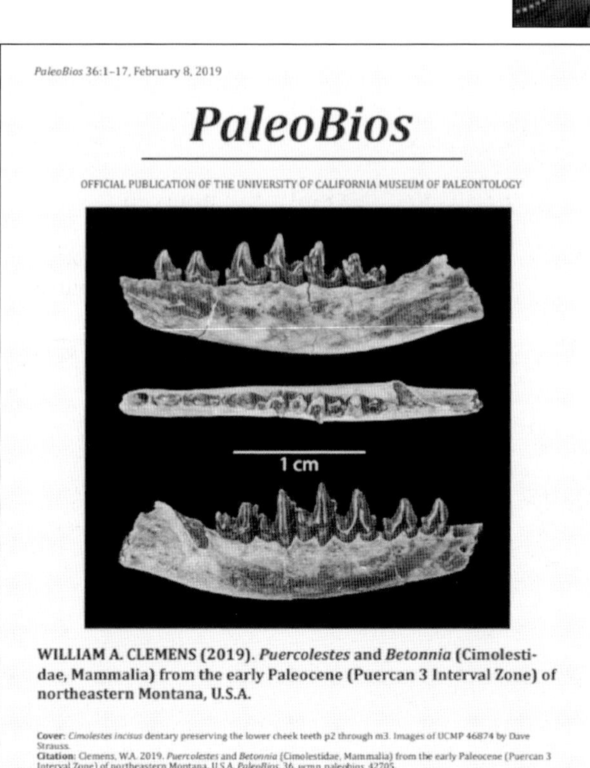

PaleoBios 36:1–17, February 8, 2019

PaleoBios

OFFICIAL PUBLICATION OF THE UNIVERSITY OF CALIFORNIA MUSEUM OF PALEONTOLOGY

1 cm

WILLIAM A. CLEMENS (2019). *Puercolestes* and *Betonnia* (Cimolestidae, Mammalia) from the early Paleocene (Puercan 3 Interval Zone) of northeastern Montana, U.S.A.

Cover: *Cimolestes incisus* dentary preserving the lower cheek teeth p2 through m3. Images of UCMP 46874 by Dave Strauss.
Citation: Clemens, W.A. 2019. *Puercolestes* and *Betonnia* (Cimolestidae, Mammalia) from the early Paleocene (Puercan 3 Interval Zone) of northeastern Montana, U.S.A. *PaleoBios*, 36. ucmp_paleobios_42705.

PaleoBios, creatively edited by Diane Erwin but handled by graduate students previously, is the official journal of UCMP. It publishes the results of research in paleontology and related fields. The journal is peer-reviewed and open access. It was first published in 1967 and now has 38 volumes. In this issue, William Clemens writes on mammals that lived soon after the extinction of the dinosaurs. (Courtesy of UCMP.)

Museum scientist (retired) Ken Finger studied and curated microfossils at UCMP. An expert on single-celled, shelled foraminifera, he documented them and geology in 60 publications and four books. Finger curated and databased more than 46,000 samples and specimens from 24,000 localities worldwide and preserved the field notes of paleontologists. He enjoyed showing microfossils through a microscope to kids. Commonly, he assisted researchers with microfossils. (Courtesy of Ken Finger.)

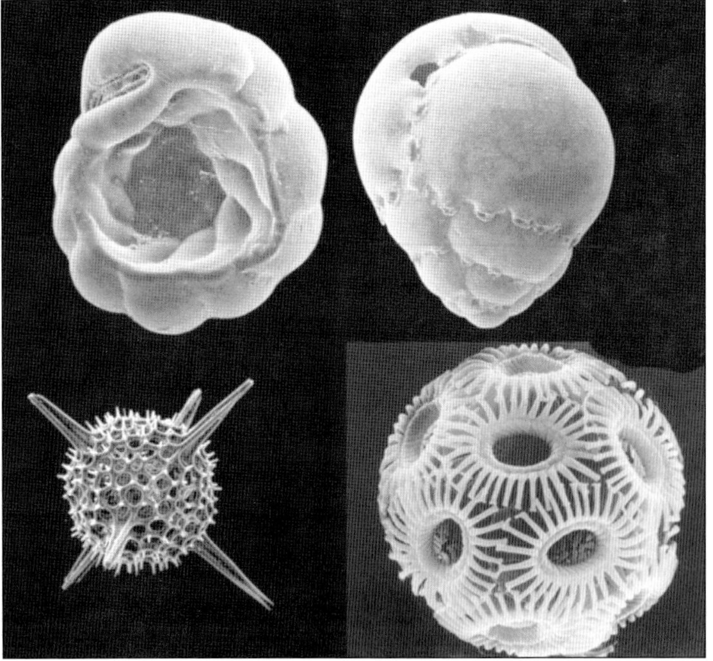

Microfossils include single-celled organisms, tiny parts of plants, animals, and pollen. Single-celled forms occur in rocks as old as 2.9 billion years. They require special preparation and microscopic techniques. Because they are smaller than a sand grain, they are best seen in scanning electron micrographs: foraminifera (top), a radiolarian (lower left), and a coccolithophorid (lower right). Six curators and their many students have studied microfossils at UCMP. (Courtesy of Ken Finger.)

Museum scientist Ashley Dineen stands in the invertebrate section of UCMP. Dineen joined UCMP in 2019, and while she specializes in marine invertebrates, her prior studies also involved vertebrate paleoecology. Her research focuses on food web structure and functional diversity dynamics during and after major environmental disturbance (climate regime transitions or mass extinction) in Paleozoic and Mesozoic paleo-communities. Currently, she works at the rehousing, curation, and web-mobilization of UCMP's Cambrian and Ordovician (~541–445 mya) marine invertebrate collection. This collection records one of the most important intervals in life's history, providing insight into early animal evolution and the rapid diversification of life in the oceans. (Courtesy of A. Dineen.)

Paleontologists and institutions have contributed to the UCMP collections starting in the days of LeConte. Since then, donations have continued unabated. T. Wayland Vaughan (left, 1870–1952), a geologist and paleontologist, directed Scripps Institution of Oceanography from 1924 to 1936. When he retired, he deposited his collection of 660 larger foraminifera in UCMP. UCLA micropaleontologists Helen Tappan and Alfred Loeblich Jr. (below, collecting in Sardinia, Italy) donated 6,000 samples collected worldwide and their library of papers to UCMP. UC Riverside gave its vertebrate fossils, the Los Angeles Natural History Museum sent a paleobotany collection, and the US Geological Survey donated a huge collection of invertebrate fossils from the West Coast and Alaska. All donations have been gratefully accepted for the value they add to UCMP's collections. (Left, courtesy of the Smithsonian Institution; below, author's collection.)

CalDay is a campus-wide event at UC Berkeley in April. UCMP, which had long presented its own annual open house, takes part in it every year. The museum is open for tours through the collections, some labs, and classrooms. The main events are in the Wallace Atrium in front of the museum entrance and under the *Tyrannosaurus rex*. These might include a preparation of a fossil or digging through sediment for fossils, an activity that kids enjoy. Usually, in a classroom, microfossils can be examined under a microscope to show the amazing variety of forms. Looking down into the atrium in 2009 (above), many visitors can be seen viewing exhibits. Below, graduate student Molly Wright discusses the evolution of a group of arthropods. Faculty curators, staff, and graduate students give lectures on a variety of topics. (Both, courtesy of UCMP Archives.)

In 1989, David Lindberg and Jere Lipps, UCMP director, wanted to put UCMP's fossil database on the internet so users could access it remotely. Rob Guralnick, a graduate student, discovered the World Wide Web. With the director's support, Guralnick and David Polly developed a web presence for UCMP. It went online in 1993 and has been updated occasionally (at left is the homepage around 2019). The website received accolades (below at right, Polly accepts a Best of the Net award from Dale Dougherty). It was also a concern: a vice chancellor told the director to take it down "because you don't know what you're doing." "Nobody does and if it turns out badly, we can unplug it" was the director's reply. Many UCMP graduate students voluntarily built the website, learning as they went. Today, it has over 14,000 pages of paleontological information. (Left, courtesy of UCMP; below, courtesy of Dave Polly.)

UC Berkeley has awarded over 425 higher degrees in paleontology since 1904. All of them are interesting and valuable studies. Shown at right is Kaitlin Maguire (PhD, 2013), who studied the paleoecology of mammals from the Mascall Formation formed in lakes and streams 15 mya in the John Day basin in Oregon. She is at the Hancock Tree standing in the Clarno Formation. The tree is permineralized, 1.6 feet in diameter, and 8.2 feet tall. It and 48 other trees were quickly preserved by a volcanic mudflow during the middle Eocene (44 mya). Douglas Long, discussing shark jaws below, received a master of arts for his 1990 thesis on fossil sharks from Seymour Island, Antarctica, and a doctorate in 1994 for a study of the historical biogeography of Pacific Ocean sharks. (Right, author's collection; below, courtesy of David Polly.)

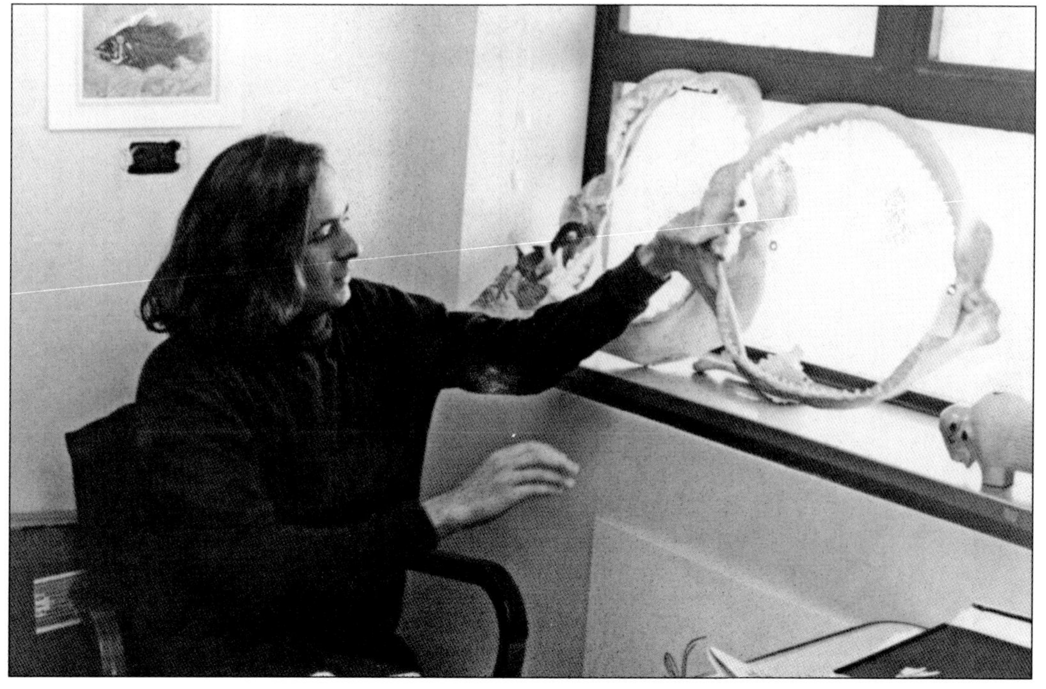

UCMP occasionally provides paleontological mitigation required under California law for earth-moving projects in the state. The Caldecott Tunnel, between the East Bay and east Contra Costa County, passes through partially fossiliferous Miocene (9 to 19 mya) shallow marine sandstones, deepwater shale, and conglomerates, sandstones, and mudstones. The first two bores were completed in 1937 (right), the third in 1964 (center), and the fourth in 2013 (left). (Author's collection.)

UCMP was engaged to prepare and curate fossils recovered in the construction of the Caldecott Tunnel's fourth bore. That excavation yielded microfossils from the shale, vertebrates (horse, camel, etc.), and leaves of *Platanus* (sycamore) and *Persea* (avocado, shown) from the sandstones and mudstones. These fossils joined the 1937 tunnel collections in UCMP. (Courtesy of UCMP.)

How many *Tyrannosaurus rex* ever lived? UCMP director Charles Marshall (right) and his students made history by answering that question in 2021. Since bigger animals have lower population densities than smaller ones, the team estimated that roughly 20,000 adolescent and adult *T. rex* lived at any one time over its geographic range. From that, the total number of *T. rex* that ever lived during its two and a half million years on Earth was calculated. The result was an astounding 2.5 billion *T. rex* roamed across western North America, ending when the dinosaurs (except for birds) became extinct 66 mya. However, given uncertainties in the analysis, the exact number could have been anywhere from 140 million to 42 billion total. These results were published in *Science Magazine* (April 16, 2021). (Above, courtesy of UCMP Archives; right, courtesy of Charles Marshall.)

Climate warming, a major problem today, has occurred multiple times in the geologic past. UCMP paleontologists examined the record at various geologic times back to 500 mya in order to understand the process of warming, how extinctions occurred during those warmings, and how those changes relate to those presently happening on Earth. The coast north of Bodega Bay, California, shows a 125,000-year-old terrace formed worldwide when the sea level was about 27 feet higher than present during a warm period. A sea-cut terrace with sea stacks and a sea cliff at the base of the hills is covered by marine gravels and sand, in places with fossils; above that, younger alluvial deposits formed after the sea level fell to 400 feet below the current level 18,000–13,000 years ago, followed by a rise again to the present level. Among the fossils are species indicating warmer water than now. These sea level oscillations are controlled by the amount of ice on the continents. When climate cools, ice grows and the sea level drops; when it warms, ice melts and the sea level rises. (Author's collection.)

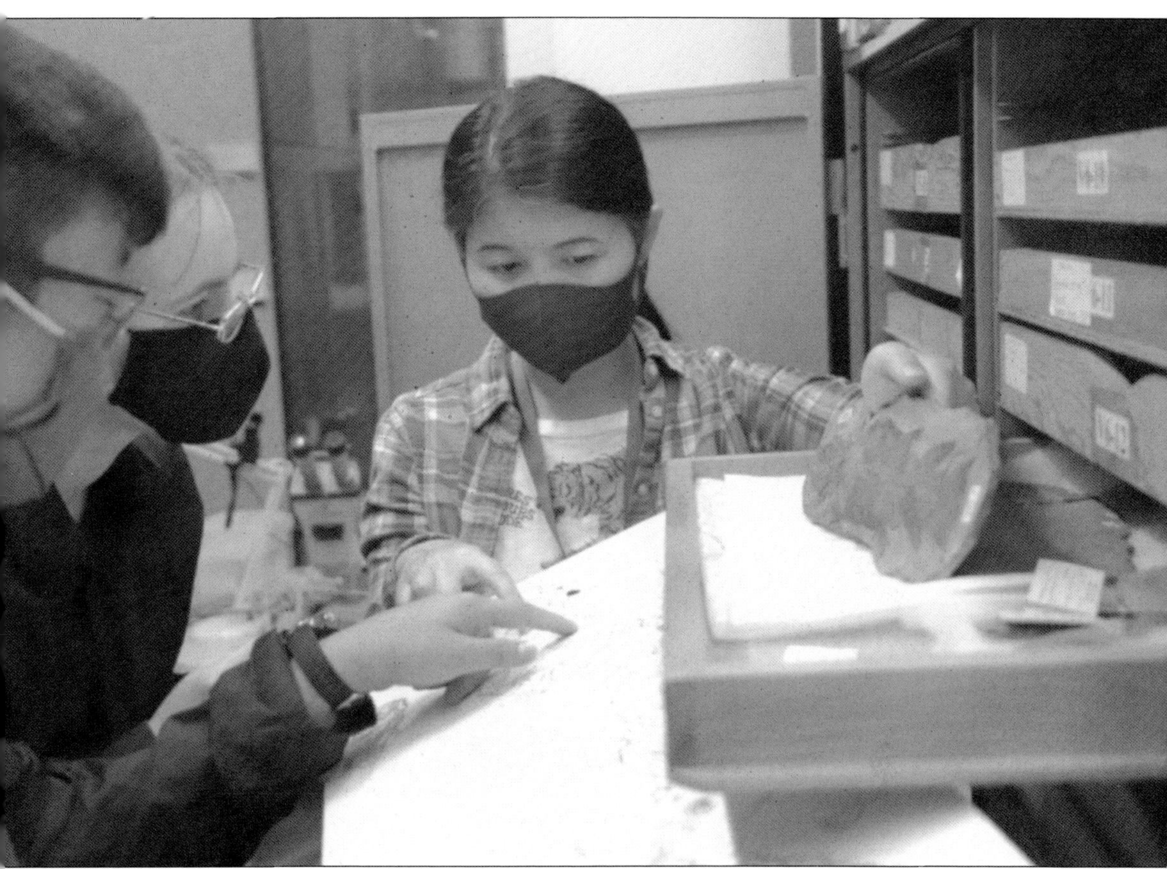

In 2020, COVID-19 struck UCMP, as it did most everything else, in mostly negative ways. World War II closed down UCMP and, for only the second time in its history, so did the pandemic. No one was allowed into the collections, labs, or other rooms, nor could they go into the field. Classes were closed. Everyone was locked down in their homes, which lacked resources and equipment to advance paleontology, except for thinking and writing. Fossil Coffee, the popular weekly seminar begun decades ago, was done remotely. With vaccines available in 2021, activities were slowly opened through December 2021. Here in September 2021, associate curator Juan Liu worked with her doctoral students Derrick Leong (left) and Jenniffer Hoeflich (center); they had shots, tested negatively for the virus, and were masked. Together, they could safely examine a 380-million-year-old (Devonian) lobed-fin fish, *Eusthenopteron*, from Nevada. UCMP is still recovering from the lockdown. (Courtesy of Jack Tseng.)

Astropaleobiologists study fossils from elsewhere in the universe. Mars (left) has long been thought to harbor alien life, but missions found none. Yet Mars possessed surface water over three billion years ago, and wherever water occurs, so does life—at least on Earth. The large valley in the center of Mars has indications of shorelines and lake beds. A region 186 miles wide (below) has possible waterways that might preserve fossils. In 2020, the *Perseverance* rover and its helicopter *Ingenuity* landed on Mars to search for fossils and have already obtained rock samples for return to Earth in 2031. A mission to Jupiter's moon Europa will search for life on its icy surface. Paleontology's and UCMP's future will be exciting and bright with new discoveries and ideas from fossils recovered not only from Earth but even from other planets. (Both, courtesy of NASA.)

Bibliography

Bedrossian, Trinda L. *The California Geological Survey: A History of California's Geological Surveys 1850–2015 with a Brief Introduction to Early California Explorations*. Sacramento, CA: California Geological Survey, Special Publication 126, 2019.

Cotter, Bill. *San Francisco's 1939–1940 World's Fair: The Golden Gate International Exposition*. Charleston, SC: Arcadia Publishing, 2021.

Le Conte, Joseph. *Elements of Geology*. New York, NY: D. Appleton and Company, 1878.

———. *Compend of Geology*. New York, NY: D. Appleton and Company, 1888.

———. *Evolution and its Relation to Religious Thought*. New York, NY: D. Appleton and Company, 1888.

Lipps, Jere H. "Success story: The history and development of the Museum of Paleontology at the University of California, Berkeley." *Proceedings of the California Academy of Sciences*, vol. 55, supplement 1, no. 9. 2004: 209–243.

Mark, Stephen E. *Preserving the Living Past: John C. Merriam's Legacy in the State and National Parks*. Berkeley, CA: University of California Press, 2005.

Miller, Loye. *Lifelong Boyhood: Recollections of a Naturalist Afield*. Berkeley, CA: University of California Press, 1950.

Stein, Barbara R. *On Her Own Terms: Annie Montague Alexander and the Rise of Science in the American West*. Berkeley, CA: University of California Press, 2001.

Stephens, Lester D. *Joseph LeConte: Gentle Prophet of Evolution*. Baton Rouge, LA: Louisiana State University Press, 1982.

Uhle, Max. "The Emeryville Shellmound." *American Archaeology and Ethnology*, vol. 7, no. 1. 1907.

Consistent with our mission to preserve history on a local level, this book was printed in South Carolina on American-made paper and manufactured entirely in the United States. Products carrying the accredited Forest Stewardship Council (FSC) label are printed on 100 percent FSC-certified paper.